SURRENDERING TO
YOURSELF

Pray as if everything depended on God.
Act as if everything depended on you.

Abraham Joshua Heschel

SURRENDERING TO YOURSELF

You Are Your Own Soul Mate

IRIS KRASNOW

miramax books

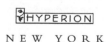

NEW YORK

Library of Congress Cataloging-in-Publication Data
ISBN: 0-7868-6913-5

10   9   8   7   6   5   4   3   2   1

To my brother and sister,
Greg and Frances

Preface

During the last year and a half, I have embarked on a journey into the soul of self—my own self and dozens of other selves. The result is this book about living from truth, about uncovering who you are, beyond your parents, marriage, children, career; beyond the expectations of your peers; beyond social games. On these pages you will meet people who have shed costumes and pretenses and unhealthy relationships that have impaired their authenticity, their potential, their ability to know themselves.

The goal of this book is for you to get real as well, to look to yourself for definition and direction, and not to the judgment of friends and lovers. You will discover how to develop immense soul power, so that when kids go to college, careers suddenly shift, family members leave or die, or you are plagued with your own illnesses, you will not come unraveled, you will carry on, head held high. Because when all else fails, we still have ourselves, and selves that are true are spiritually indestructible.

The book is divided into three parts: Who Are You?, Who Do You Want to Be?, and Surrendering to Yourself. Within these divisions I deal with every human emotion and condition imaginable: from birth, death, marriage, child-bearing, divorce, aging, faith, plastic surgery. These categories are flushed out in eighteen subsections, with titles such as "Excavating Your Truth," "Discarding Old Selves," "What God Can Do for You," and "Can Botox Fix Your Soul?"

Like my two previous books, *Surrendering to Motherhood* and *Surrendering to Marriage*, I work in three ways as a journalist, layering language with personal narrative, interviews, and passages from other literature. This is the last volume in the *Surrendering* trilogy.

Here are several of the voices who serve as travel guides on this voyage into the center of self: Luis, a man who has carried the HIV virus for seventeen years but remains asymptomatic of AIDS; Natalie, eight months pregnant and seated in the passenger seat next to her husband when a drunk truck driver careened into their Jeep and killed him; Gary Caruso, afflicted with a rare and incurable cancer of the palate who has been told by puzzled doctors they have no idea how long he will live; Suzi, the daughter of blue-collar parents whose rich and randy husband transported her into a world of furs, expensive cars, and a lavish home, but the dirty secret inside that gilded 21-year-old marriage was a lonely wife, and her dread of divorce because it would crush their picture-perfect image; and Barbara, a woman rejected at age nineteen by the Eileen Ford Agency who fifty years later resurrected her dream of stalking a runway, and now at seventy-two has a flourishing modeling career.

You will also hear from Ben Bradlee, the longtime executive editor of the *Washington Post*, who reflects on life at 81, and on the climb down from his position as one of the most powerful and revered chiefs of international journalism.

PREFACE

Most subjects chose to use their real names, but a few asked to be identified with pseudonyms, which they got to pick. In cases where sources preferred anonymity, some identifying details have also been changed, such as what jobs they held and where they live. Yet every sentence of every interview is true to the bone; these are unaltered stories that shoot straight from their hearts.

This guide to living with purpose, urgency, and passion could not have been possible without many purposeful, urgent, and passionate coaches and friends. First off, I'd like to thank Jonathan Burnham and Susan Mercandetti, top editors at Miramax Books, for believing in me time and time again, and for making my literary dreams happen. This is my third book that has been edited by Susan Dalsimer, and I am enormously grateful for this remarkable woman, who never fails to push me into raw honesty and to sharpen my writing.

I would also like to thank my agent Jan Miller, a friend of twenty-two years, who knows how to move with my ideas, where to move, and when to make the move. Kristin Powers, another talented mover and shaper, has my immense gratitude as well. Kristin is the person at Miramax who oversees the actual building of the book, from deadlines to page construction to jacket design. And to my assistant Laura Hollon, I am deeply appreciative of the hours and devotion you put into this project.

My books on life and love could never unfold without the closeness and solidity of family. I'd like to thank my father, Theodore Krasnow, who died in 1986, and my very alive mother, Helene Krasnow, for giving me strength and optimism and for instilling in me from childhood a passion for reading and communicating. My husband, Chuck Anthony, has been a partner in all ways since our wedding in March of 1988, and I thank him, and love him eternally for his commitment and unwavering support. He has also given me four amazing children, Theo and Isaac and Jack and Zane, boys I thank along with their father for loving me and providing me with such great material for my books. And to my treasured circle of vintage girlfriends, you have my awe and appreciation for knowing instinctively what wives and mothers need most of all, and that is to sit around with other women and laugh and vent.

Finally, to the generous and honest people who allowed me to root around their psyches for this book, I owe you everything. Your stories of surrender and self-realization illuminate every page. And to Ruth Berlin and Greg Nolan, thanks for helping me hear my own truth and the whisperings of the Almighty.

Who Are You?

Rebirth After Miscarriage

I am forty-seven, and a few months ago I found out I was pregnant. It was a shock, although I certainly know how babies are made and I know if you're not careful, you may make one. But it's been eight years since our twins were born, and we're not always careful, yet I still nearly had to be picked up off the floor as the "yes" line turned a fluorescent red on the home pregnancy test. I was ecstatic.

Before my husband Chuck had the chance to move from shock to ecstasy with me, I miscarried. How could this happen? I was so sad, so sure that this baby was meant to be. I would have loved another child, another boy if that was in the stars, or our first girl. What a gift, a daughter to inherit my silver jewelry, collected over forty years.

Our four sons—big boys, ages twelve, ten, and eight-year-old twins—are playing outside, one at the basketball hoop, two on the swings, one drawing with lime green chalk on the sidewalk. It's taken a long time to get to the point where having four children loose in the backyard doesn't require close supervision. As I scrub burnt cheddar from the pan in which I made macaroni and cheese, cramping from miscarrying, I am relieved, yet morose. Relieved we don't have to start over, with diapers and ear infections and sleepless nights. Regretful that I won't have an armful of warm baby, so soft you can't stop kissing and touching him, nestled, nursing, mine. Regretful that I don't have one more life to create and to shape, one more chance to sit with other mothers in my kitchen, talking and laughing over the silliest of infant talk: which kid likes a pacifier, which kid doesn't poop enough, which kid sleeps the night, which kid has never slept a day in his two-month life.

Surveying our sons outside, Chuck says, "See, we have the perfect family. They can take care of themselves. Why would we want more children?" And with that I start to cry, because indeed, why would we want more, but why would we not? I already miss the clingy, love-Mommy phase.

Although I know how blessed I am to have four healthy children, still I can't shake the sadness. I am aware that we already have the "perfect family," as my husband puts it. But losing a baby doesn't feel perfect. I need to move through this. So why can't I?

After we first found out about the pregnancy, Chuck, in one of our many incredulous conversations, shook his head and said: "We can't start a child on a new life right now. When he is in kindergarten we'll be in our fifties." I went to sit alone on the hill outside my kitchen, a spot under a big pine tree where I had nursed four babies. I was remembering the birth of Theo, quick and easy, and Isaac, an emergency C-section because he was in the breech position. Then came twins Jack and Zane, eleven minutes apart, a natural delivery of two robust boys. Now, one more. There was a spiritual rightness to the timing of this conception, or else why would it have occurred?

I am still wistful about what happened and didn't happen, yet I have come to see that while this miscarriage marked my official end of childbearing, it also marked the official beginning of something I had yet to do—to birth myself. I had been birthing children and birthing books, birthing hundreds of newspaper and magazine articles. Now it was time to bring myself fully into the world, as a woman not attached to needy babies but as my unadorned self.

One of the joys of mothering young children is that you get to pour yourself into others while putting off dealing with your own issues. When I wrote *Surrendering to Motherhood*, our kids were four and under and I was an earth mother who was hugely relieved to be grinding vegetables into baby food rather than spinning around in journalism or romance, or in puzzling about life, as I did when I was single. I could focus on babies who needed to be fed and changed and nuzzled, and I could forget about me.

That phase is long gone. With children who are now self-sufficient and in school all day, I have no infants to get lost in, no tiny bodies to hide behind. I pack their lunches, drive them to school, then go home to an empty, quiet house. However demanding it is to tend to an infant, one more baby would have been easy in many ways, because I could avoid the hard work of facing myself.

I live in a county where large families are everywhere; it must be something in our drinking water. Often, when the Anthony tribe is seated in a restaurant, parents with five or six children will be next to us. I understand why some women keep having babies. It's a way to hold on to our fertile youth and stay distracted from our own selves. I am that woman who could keep having more and more children. But the spiritual masters knew better this time. They knew I was on the cusp of a new self, a self apart from the mother of many. So I'm not only mourning the loss of babies in our home, I'm mourning the mama who for twelve years, has been hoisting chubby children, dunking them in the Atlantic waves, wiping their noses, soothing them to sleep after bad dreams, a person so attached to them that I became them. Alas, new motherhood for this old mama wasn't to be; I would bring forth into the world not another child, but an original self.

Tonight I have taken twelve-year-old Theo out alone to Tsunami sushi restaurant, where he tells the waiter he'd like a California roll, "with real crab, not fake crab," as if he's thirty. As he expertly mixes up wasabi with soy and maneuvers his chopsticks to his mouth without spilling a grain of rice, I get a sharp image of him at three when he wore a polyester Superman Halloween costume for nearly one year, over his pajamas and over his clothes, refusing to take it off except for his bath. Tonight we're on a date, and Theo's got his collar turned up on his white polo shirt, which is tucked into jeans, and he is talking about wanting to live in Los Angeles someday because he likes the atmosphere there.

And I'm missing him already because he may turn out to be like his mother and, indeed, pick a college in California because he likes the atmosphere there. Two years later, Isaac will be gone; in another two years, Jack and Zane follow. And who will I be when I'm not mothering children? The vision of our dining room table with me at one end, Chuck at the other, and no one in between already leaves a lonely sting.

Who *are* you apart from your mothering? Do you know that person well? I say we try and birth that new self while we still have our parenting jobs so that when the kids are gone, we aren't flailing. You know the old saying: Look for a new job while you still have your old one, so you're standing on firm ground while you're scouting. Giving birth to ourselves is our ultimate, hardest achievement because we must do it alone. There's nothing except what's inside of us to brace ourselves against.

So I suppose it's time to do what I've been unable to do, give away some of the baby clothes stashed in piles in the attic: the buttery cotton T-shirts that snap at the crotch, the sweaters emblazoned with cowboys or Goofy. It's time, finally, it's time. Theo wears a size 10½ men's shoe, and one of the eight-year-old twins is taller than my mother. I'll keep some of the clothes for my grandchildren and pack up the rest and give them to other mothers who have real babies in their homes, and not just howling memories, like me.

Yes, a new baby is a way to avoid what must happen to all of us, and that is, to face our aloneness. Let me shake you awake, like I've been shaken awake. Let me elucidate the importance of confronting our stuff midstream in life rather than wait until we're too old to change. Because if we can learn how to be content just hanging out with our real selves at the age of forty-five, then we can have four more decades of peace within. So start the process today—know thyself, love thyself—and understand that although our lives may now be filled with adoring children, those children are separate from us. Our self is our sole possession. We've gotten tremendous satisfaction from birthing babies and birthing projects at work. Yet there is nothing more satisfying or profound than beginning the process of being born again, not in the Lord, though the Lord is part of it, but in the chrysalis of your soul.

I drop my four children off at school and have to practically wrestle each of them to get a kiss goodbye. They run to their classrooms without even a backward glance, sons who used to clutch at my knees so I wouldn't leave. No more babies, it's only me and my car this morning, and the lingering odor of boys who won't think of their mother all day unless I forgot to put cookies in their lunch. And I turn on an old Fleetwood Mac tape and their sexy rocking makes me think of being fifteen and frolicking on Oak Street Beach in Chicago, of the surreal and seductive atmosphere of California in college, of riding horses, of birthing my next self.

EXCAVATING YOUR TRUTH

Living your truth takes excavation and examination of gut passions and primal character, like an archaeologist on a dig. You must sift through layers and layers of false selves to get to your naked essence, through capillaries and bones into the marrow of your being, into the unmasking of the soul. Soul is the fluid spirit of self that is pure truth, pure you, untarnished and undiluted by time and experiences, the link with God and eternity. By strengthening and transforming in the marrow of self, you become a person who begins to trust her own voice, her own gut, her own reach, her own intuition.

My first book, *Surrendering to Motherhood*, is about yielding to the higher power of your commitment to raising children; *Surrendering to Marriage* is about yielding to the sacred promise you make on your wedding day to stick with your partner through heaven and hell and imperfections. *Surrendering to Yourself*, the last in the trilogy, is the most difficult and most important surrender. It is about mustering up the courage to yield to your true self and embrace that flawed person, a process I am still in the midst of but getting better at every day. It is about discarding old selves that are disingenuous, crafted over time to form protective shields or to placate others or to get ahead. It is about boldly realizing the time is *now* to live your dreams, to quit jobs you hate, to sever unhealthy relationships, to plug back into childhood passions, to figure out who God is and what She/He can open up for you. Surrendering to yourself means facing your death, even if you have never been sicker than a bout with the flu.

This surrender to self is not a selfish pursuit. Self-knowledge and the discovery of clarity from within means the creation of a person who can best love and serve others.

Surrendering to yourself means coming fully unleashed, unconditionally and explosively. Next time you sing "Wild thing, I think I love you," you should be singing it to yourself. Joan of Arc spoke of being true to her "inner voices," to values firmly held. We should all aspire to letting our inner voices, and not others' voices, shout directions for how to live.

Many people do not discover who they genuinely are until they've been hit with a tragedy and are forced to come crashing into themselves at Lamborghini speed: Your wife leaves you for a chiseled hunk fifteen years younger. Your remaining parent dies. You are unrelentingly depressed and without direction when the last child goes off to college. You lose a longstanding job. Your blood test comes back HIV positive. You miscarry in middle age, your last-chance baby.

I wrote my first two books from the trenches. The one on motherhood was composed when I quit my job to take care of four children, ages four and under, and was thrashing in the transition. The second book was an eyes-wide-open look into how tough it is to sustain a marriage, written from the heart of my own rocking and rolling union. This time around, I am gazing at my subject from a distance. I am not sick. My spouse has not run off. I still have one parent. An empty nest is years away. Yet I am compelled to get a jump on this process of surrendering to myself, before I've been pushed over the edge, because I know the edges loom closer, that precipice beckons, that age and time brings illness and death and change.

I want to, I need to, be ready. In writing this book, I hope to propel myself and like-minded readers who are striding healthily into middle age to unravel ourselves, and surrender, long before a crisis hits. We should be thinking life-lifts, not face-lifts, and realize that when we get crevices in our faces, Botox cannot fix our souls. We should at every age make sure we remain connected to our childhood passions, sports, and other forms of play that make us feel youthful and hopeful and alive.

I started taking tumbling and gymnastics when I was a toddler and loved it immediately. I was doing the splits at age five, and flips at ten; I was a cheerleader at fifteen and still do stunts off the diving board. When I want to get my children's attention, I fly across the backyard in a series of cartwheels and splits. The other day, ten-year-old Isaac asked, "Mommy, when you're eighty, do you think you will still be able to do the splits?" "Of course I will," I answered. And I will if I'm alive, because I refuse to squelch my spirit that is still child just because I'm a grown-up now. I've taught the boys how to play jacks and we often play on our living room floor.

In 1986, as a feature writer for United Press International, I interviewed artist Louise Nevelson in her New York studio. Nevelson, eighty-six at the time, was wearing a flowing batik wrap, crushed velvet pants, and black patent leather shoes. She was part gypsy, part queen, and 100 percent present, spunky and deft. This matriarch of twentieth-century sculpture, who is known for her welded steel sculptures that rise as high as seventy feet, told me she was as sharp at eighty-six as when she was the captain of her high school basketball team.

"I can get drunk now, and say I want to throw something

and hit a spot on the ceiling, I'll hit it," she said, pointing to the ceiling. "It's more than good aim or good physical coordination—it's something else in the mind."

She paused to take a sip of chilled apple cider, then added: "I always knew exactly who I was and exactly what I wanted, and at my age I still know what I want. I've never changed in my life.

"I knew from childhood that I was going to be an artist."

I have played back Nevelson's line "I always knew who I was and exactly what I wanted" time and time again in my own life, and while I've tried to remain true to the passions of my youth, when I met this sure-footed octogenarian I was unsure of who I was and what the future held. Single and thirty-one, I was career-bitten and adrenaline laced but hankering for deeper roots and a different life. Wanting a mate and children, I had instead a glamorous beat interviewing famous people from Yoko Ono to Billy Graham, but those rushes didn't last; they were like soap bubbles in the air. And here was Louise Nevelson, a rock, unflinching and serene, a follower of Krishnamurti, the master who believed that truth can be ours only by quieting our minds and discovering, moment to moment, what he calls the ways of the self. As Nevelson spoke to me about her spiritual guide I had anything but a quiet mind and was not in the moment; I was flashing forward to the day I could stop dating, make some babies, and settle down. I loved my work, but work is work and life is life, and the life part seemed flimsy, empty.

Today I am filled with family and life, anchored by roots, history, and a future with grandchildren. Having a permanent base allows me to fly into another sphere of self, one who is not chasing around for missing pieces but is feeling whole, satiated, daring. More and more, I am able to do what Krishnamurti suggests we do, to completely stop inwardly so the mind can become peaceful and clear. From that place of stillness, you can focus on who you are, the passions of your soul, what you were meant to do. You then become grounded in self-esteem and enduring emotional success, far more important than tailoring a career so you can earn a big salary. Yet those with passion and focus and perseverance often end up reaping monetary rewards as well.

Don't stop doing the splits or shooting baskets or playing jacks if that's what you once loved to do. We should never be afraid to be exactly who we are at all ages and stages, fully flexed, 100 percent human beings who operate out of honesty, people who dare to be outrageous, no matter the consequences.

"Conforming to social expectations and to a persona that doesn't reflect our deep inner self is like going through life wearing shoes that are too tight," writes Kathleen A. Brehony in *Awakening at Midlife.* "In too tight shoes you can walk—but you can't dance. And at midlife, the soul is demanding to dance."

When the soul demands to dance, we are propelled into a glorious wildness, such as taking aerobatic flying lessons at forty or ballet lessons at forty-five; becoming a fashion model at seventy or a weight lifter in your eighties. I'm talking about never again acting in a manner the French call *contre-coeur,* "against the wishes of the heart."

I'm thinking about an architect in his sixties, with three grown kids, and a wife of thirty-five years. He is in love with a male colleague, but will not come out until his mother, a steely patrician type, dies. He and everyone around him are suffering—his wife, his children—twisted in a lie, a charade. His perfect-to-the-eye family, with impeccable looks and breeding, will be altered by this truth, but it is the truth, and illusions need to burst open. His mother will survive, everyone will. Some of the architect's loved ones will even be proud of him, for having the guts to be real.

Being real is a scary thing. In the words of Carl Jung: "There is no birth of consciousness without pain." But to have integrity, the highest of qualities, you must shoot straight with others and come clean with yourself. Do you act in accordance with the dictates of your heart? Do you speak your mind? I do more and more, and not everybody likes it, and more and more, I could care less. I love it when friends and acquaintances are direct with me, telling me if I have inadvertently hurt them or overlooked them or wronged them in any other way. Then I get to apologize if I'm at fault or explain a misunderstanding, and we can move on. And I believe those people in turn appreciate my own tendency to be absolutely straightforward when I have my own complaints with them.

My son Theo just completed a season playing a sport for one of our county A-teams of twelve-year-old boys. His coach used intimidation to shape up his team, and they lost many of their games. Red-faced and angry, he would routinely single out a child and scream at him, making him feel like a loser. Some kids would melt into tears. My son was his target several times. His tirades were wrenching for the parents to watch and a horrible example of adult behavior for the children. But no dad or mom wanted to face off with the coach for fear his wrath would only worsen.

After the last game, a loss, the coach badgered his team badly instead of thanking them for the season. Theo came to me, face down, voice cracking: "I gave him my hand to shake, and he looked away. I never got to show him what a good player I could be. You can't play well when someone is always telling you what you're doing wrong and not what you're doing right." My blood boiled when Theo said that he felt that the coach took his confidence away. I told him no one could take his confidence away if he believes in himself, and that he should, because he is a strong player.

Since no pain is greater than the pain a parent feels when her kid has been beaten down, I told Theo to wait a few minutes, that I'd be right back. I then cornered the coach and told him that my husband and I work very hard at building self-esteem in our four sons by giving them positive reinforcement as well as constructive criticism. I felt the vein in my neck throbbing as I went on to say that he had been battering the team's self-esteem, not building it, like a coach should do. And that when an athlete feels strong, he does better on the field, so why the hell would he rarely commend them for a job well done?

His response was snarly, not apologetic.

Years ago I would not have had the guts to confront one

of the most formidable youth coaches in the county; I would have wanted him to like me more than I would have wanted to risk his thinking I was a ranting, over-emotional mother. Today I don't care what this man thinks of me. I care what my son thinks of himself. Today, when my heart wells up with sadness and rage, words spill out, and it feels wonderful. It's good to release thoughts that are leaden and crushing; that's a key principle of surrendering to yourself, to never allow toxic energy to rip up your insides. Doctors tell us to get things off our chests, to lighten up, lessening the chance of heart attacks and stress-related illnesses. When you lighten your load, you can get on with things that really matter.

When you're honest with yourself, it flows naturally that you are honest with others. And if someone finds your honesty offensive, it's best for both parties if they clear out of your lives.

Too often we seek a certain relationship or travel to an exotic destination for no reason other than to escape ourselves. Yet, yourself is something you will never be able to shake, no matter how much you soft-pedal yourself to suit other people or how many vacations you take in search of happiness. In the words of the Buddha, you will be like "a monkey who jumps from tree to tree, never finding fruit—from life to life, never finding peace." So you may as well stop right now and listen, really listen, to what's going on inside. You are who you are, and from that, there is no escape.

That voice of truth will haunt you wherever you go. Better to embrace it, heed it, surrender to the higher power of your soul. By doing this now rather than later, you are giving yourself the freedom to become a self that is centered and resilient, a rock to fall back on when your world suddenly shifts.

If you're awake and honest about yourself every step of the way, when someone you love dies or leaves you for another, you can be steadied by that rock within. Everything around you may be fleeting, but you will always have you, and that's a lot. I want to be ready, I need to be ready, when my four boys are all out the door.

I had no trouble finding sources to interview for *Surrendering to Yourself*. In fact, it was easy, they came to me serendipitously, as they did when I was writing my earlier books on motherhood and marriage that focused on a generational angst that lots of people were experiencing along with me. When I had four kids in diapers and had left a big journalism job, I met many other mothers grappling with the shift from being women of the world to mothers at home. In the earlier years of our marriage, when we did more rocking than rolling, I encountered countless other husbands and wives who expected soul-mate happiness and instead got loneliness and confusion. When I mentioned the title *Surrendering to Yourself*, often people would get a glint in their eye, nod and sigh, then tell me that's precisely what they are going through or need to go through. That is, resurrecting lost selves, discarding illusory selves, learning to love themselves.

For example, the owner of a designer accessory business,

who you will hear from later in the book, told me she knows the power of surrendering painfully well. Her first marriage of eleven years, a union with a "perfect man," ended when her husband was killed in a car accident by a drunk truck driver. She was seated in the front seat next to him, eight months pregnant with their first child. This woman, who was thirty-five at the time, broke her pelvis, lost her teeth, but came out alive. Their baby daughter was born healthy. Today, after a bout with alcohol abuse and two subsequent failed marriages, this woman will tell you: "I have been to rock-bottom and back, and depended on too many people for self-worth. Finally I am anchored in myself."

From true surrender to self comes a sustained knowing that beneath every black internal cloud there are brilliant shards of sunlight. And as that light spills out onto others, your power sparks their power. From true surrender comes an ability to accept every imperfection of your being. It took me a long time to admit that I am a broken being who will never be perfect: that I can be irrational and impatient, that I will never look like Rita Hayworth (to me, the most gorgeous woman). But I have grown to accept my brokenness, some of which can never be fixed, and have grown to love and be able to laugh at the real person I am. From surrender comes faith and an opening to the spiritual potential in all of the universe. And from this ultimate connection, you can be the best parent, the best spouse, the best human possible. Once you come to know who you really are, behind costumes and personalities, you are ready for anything.

By surrendering to yourself, you can be your most benevolent, most passionate, most indefatigable. Anchored by self-love, nobody can knock you down. By surrendering, you are taking the bull by the horns rather than being bull-dozed. We become people who don't search out answers from friends or lovers; rather we begin to rely solely on the compass in our hearts and the map in our souls.

For *Surrendering to Marriage*, I spoke to hundreds of people in various stages of marriage, from blissful newly-weds to jaded baby boomers having affairs to couples celebrating golden anniversaries. And what I heard over and over again was hostile partners blaming husbands and wives for their own malaise. What became clear, and became one of the catalysts for this book, was that those accusing fingers were pointed in the wrong direction: We are in charge of our own fulfillment and satisfaction. No one else can make us happy; we must do that for ourselves.

Bernice Land baby-sat for our sons when they were younger, and has been a housekeeper and nanny for most of her sixty-one years, starting at age fifteen, when her mother died and she quit school to care for ten younger siblings. Bernice has a beautiful alto-tenor voice and has always made time to attend twice-a-week choir practices and sing gospel every Sunday at church. A single mother who raised three children on her own, she has never been able to quit her day job to work solely on developing her music, which is her primary passion. But hurling out gospel songs keeps her linked to her true self and makes her work during the week more tolerable. As Bernice says: "I love God. I love singing. It gets me to my soul. That's what keeps me from getting depressed."

Whatever your job or your circumstances, don't abandon the passion of your soul! A local podiatrist, Lyle Modlin, has magnificent photographs displayed on the walls throughout his office. There are shots he took of sites spanning Florida's Sanibel Island to Jerusalem, and they are of *National Geographic* quality. He says photography is what he loves more than any other trade, but with a wife and three young children, he can't abandon his medical profession. Yet he has never abandoned his camera, and he has never stopped growing as a photographer, a craft he has loved since his high school days.

Staying connected to or reconnecting with the passions of your youth keeps you fortified, fascinated and fascinating. No matter how much we love another, no other person can give you this gift of life. Your strength lies within, rooted in your soul, that spirit that fills every appendage and pore and is the architect of your potential, your character.

Surrendering to yourself is about realizing that your soul mate is not the person you are living with or a mystery person out there, waiting to unravel you, discover you. You can love a partner completely; he or she can trigger ecstasy and lust. But an act as intimate as the mating of the soul can happen only internally; it's a dance that is exquisitely private between you and yourself. You have already met your most reliable, most intuitive, most trustworthy friend. And that is the person in the mirror, someone who may have graying hair, furrows between the eyebrows, a softening middle, lines above the lips. Before you choose to eradicate the etchings of time with visits to physicians wielding needles and knives, know that looking younger doesn't guarantee you'll feel any better. You will still be you.

In the early 1980s, I lived in Texas, working as the fashion writer for the now-defunct *Dallas Times Herald*. I became friends with a wrinkly, confident white-haired woman of sixty-four who owned one of the city's most prestigious women's clothiers. She used to shake her head and cluck her tongue when customers would walk by with tight faces and huge stand-up breasts.

"Honey, they are fixin' the wrong thing," she would mutter under her breath. "They should be fixin' their insides." Indeed, when you are perpetually working on your insides, you will not fall apart when your beauty starts to fade. How I look is not who I am, and that's a great thing to get, because there are lots of times I don't like the way I look.

Insides last. Looks do not, even in the hands of the most artistic of surgeons. Surgeons are mere humans, not magicians who can make a lifetime disappear. Surrendering to vanity, and allowing self-realization to wither, means letting a superficial obsession flatten your spiritual core. It's a disease that no collagen or Botox or fat-sucking machine can ever cure.

You get your eyes lifted, and just when you're done healing from that procedure, you feel a need to get your lips plumped or your neck tightened to go with your new eyes. A year later, you return for cheek implants and liposuction of the thighs. Where do you stop? This is a game no patient or doctor can ever win, this desperate race against time. Weeks turn into months, and months turn into decades, and decades weather flesh; this is a fact of life. Realize now, whatever age you are, that the fountain of youth needs to be replenished from within.

The people who do best with plastic surgery are the ones who have already fixed the right thing inside, the ones who know that lifted eyes and lifted boobs only lift the spirit and body temporarily, but do not resurrect a sagging life.

Do you know anyone with an empty life who was emotionally and spiritually filled by multiple cosmetic surgeries? Living in Dallas from 1980 to 1984, a town where physical perfection and material riches are often worshiped, my own focus was turned more outward than inward. Single and in my twenties and covering the fashion beat, I was surrounded by so many perfect wardrobes and perfect bodies and perfect parties that it drove me to seek my own wrong brand of perfect for a while, and to suffer from misplaced priorities. I have kept diaries since high school, and always write in New Year's resolutions. Topping the list of twelve items scribbled at dawn on January 1st, 1983, in my Texas apartment overlooking Central Expressway was "Lose five pounds and keep working out." Coming in last was "Get to know Iris and love and accept her."

I remember being mesmerized by Dr. John Barnett, one of the busiest plastic surgeons in town, while I interviewed him for a *Times Herald* article. In a thick drawl from his Marlin, Texas, home ground, he told me how he has "rebuilt people, from top to bottom. It's a turn-on for me to take something that's okay, but not really great, and make it beautiful." I stared at my barely size B chest as he tossed me a grapefruit-sized implant that felt soft and real, like a Jell-O balloon. Two of these babies could be mine, I fantasized. He told me to call one of his former patients—a *Playboy* bunny—for some quotes for my newspaper story and for inspiration should I choose to go under his knife.

"He's just sooooo good," gushed this twenty-five-year-old bunny, who went from what she described as a saggy C to a perky D. "I used to always turn my back to the mirror when I dressed. Now, I can't stop looking at myself. I don't even have to wear a bra. They stand up by themselves."

She then went on to disclose that her boyfriend "bought them for her," that he wanted them as much as she did, perhaps more. My visions of a full C cup for myself came to a halt as I realized not only did my barely Bs already stand up by themselves, but that I too might be fixing the wrong thing for the wrong reason. Bigger boobs, gotten while you are unattached and looking for love, are something you generally use to entice the opposite sex, and that is not why I wanted a man to feel attracted to me.

I wanted him to be drawn to my soul, my essence. But I was rapidly realizing, at age twenty-seven, that I had yet to tackle the massive and essential job of knowing my own soul, the stuff in the deepest place. I knew I was a writer, and I was passionate about my work; but the self beyond journalism, boyfriends and workouts had yet to be thoroughly explored. We all have a moment in our lives when we know it's time to discard old selves and get on with things, and that was my moment, in gilded Dallas, where the flash of self-realization suddenly started blinding me.

Dr. Barnett shared with me that he gets "such a kick out of seeing his ladies come back to get their stitches out and they've got on a tube top and they've got their shoulders thrown back and a grin all over their face." And I thought later, while reviewing my notes from the interview, that I wanted to become a woman who has her shoulders thrown back and a grin on her face because of how she feels about herself, not how she looks in the mirror.

"You're gonna find that you're as beautiful as you feel," promises Carole King in the song "Beautiful," and she's got that right.

Lately, what I want more than anything is to feel beautiful from within, to excavate my own truth. In struggling to answer the question "Who am I?" I trail centuries of philosophers, psychologists, religious leaders and waves of common citizens whose central quest has been to find their purpose, their place, their essence. My own twisted journey to know self and love self accelerated as a Stanford student living in the Bay Area in the mid-1970s amid an exploding human-potential movement. I explored yoga, Transcendental Meditation, Buddhism, est, gradations of Judaism and feminism. There are stacks of beat-up books in my office that have pushed me along the path, from the writings of

Ram Dass and Carl Jung and Mother Teresa to Rollo May's *Man's Search for Himself.*

However compelling these texts are and insightful these scribes are, in the end it is you, and it is I, who must figure out things for ourselves—our values, aspirations, the meaning of integrity. Or in the words of the Buddha: "Although I have shown you the means of liberation, you must know that it depends on you alone." And so I write this book not to show you who you are, but as a mirror in which you can face yourself, and see what you need to see. This book is an opportunity, a dare, to disrobe down to the particles of your psyche.

My own mission to know myself and feel strong and powerful from within has taken years of unraveling, but I am getting there, at forty-seven, finally, thankfully. I have had great mentors, an honest husband, piles of diaries that do not lie and a longtime circle of wise-women friends to rely on. But the kick through the door into my actual self came from my own foot, my own urgency, my own mistakes. I have loved the wrong people, hurt the wrong people, worried too much about losing five pounds. I have been selfish at the wrong times and selfless at the wrong times, and have counted on other people to transport me into their worlds so I could leave myself behind.

Yet I wouldn't wish away any of my missteps made throughout the haze of youth or during my active dating years. Because these stumbles that come from searching for identity in deceptive gurus or far-flung adventures or

Mr. Wrong relationships taught me that you cannot find yourself in others or by scampering around the world. You find yourself by embarking on the most profound of adventures, the journey inward; by being still and alone and honest with yourself. This is where I am right now, seeking a center that brings not quick hits of joy, but an eternal ride, the birth of true being.

Despite ascending job titles and proliferating material goods and relationships gathered through time, you are all you ever really own. Friends come and go. Objects break, even expensive cars. Family members die. Careers peter out. You come into this world alone, through a dark birth canal. And although the decades of your life are filled with light and crowds and journeys, it is only you who you take from place to place, it is only you who will never leave you, it is only you who holds you up when what's going on around you weighs you down.

And it's only you who can nudge you to become the person you were meant to be all along. Being revered by others is never as crucial as the respect you hold for yourself. When you keep score on your accomplishments, and stop gauging who you are by others' scorecards, nothing can crack your self-esteem. And it's only with self-esteem and self-love that you can become the person who leaps out of bed each morning, eager to tackle the day, the person who realizes that passion and perseverance are everything.

As much as we drum into our children that to do their best they must persevere, I have found with our own sons, that being propelled to peak performance can happen more effectively from watching outsiders they admire. Four summers ago, when three of our four kids couldn't swim and refused to learn how to from me, we picked a baby-sitter who had just completed her freshman year at Harvard University as the top butterflyer on the swim team. Training with the irrepressible Kirra Brandon, our scared swimmers turned into cocky sea animals.

Brandon's powerhouse stroke, back muscles rippling, will forever be etched in the minds of our boys, who try and imitate her to this day every time they get into a pool. I often asked Brandon about her own childhood, what her parents did to make her succeed. Brandon said that her father had quit high school in his native Australia to learn the trade of sign-painting, his occupation to this day. Her mother left a teaching career to stay home and raise two children.

"My parents never measured our success by whether we were the best or the first," recalled Brandon, now a sophomore in medical school at the University of Maryland. "They defined success by how hard you tried each day. When I was young, I wasn't even a fast swimmer. In fact, I was pretty slow. But I kept at it because I knew if I didn't give up, I would get better and better."

PLUGGING INTO YOUR PASSION

Who are you? Is the life you are leading real or fake? Your truth is etched in your beginning. Plugging into talents and passions that are spiritually right, those that spring from our primal selves, often starts when we are young, encouraged by adults who are paying attention.

In my girlhood house of green shutters and white brick in Oak Park, Illinois, I discovered a passion for language that would be the seed of who I would become. I was blessed with parents and teachers who recognized that passion and pushed me to work harder, to get published, to never give up on my dreams.

I have known since the first grade at Horace Mann School, under the withering stare of Miss Bernice Steger, that deciphering words and writing sentences was what I most enjoyed. Miss Steger would stand at the blackboard next to the window, the sunlight sending shimmers through her gray French twist, writing two- and three-letter words from the Dick and Jane series. Those days of autumn, more than forty years ago, when letters became words and I began to read are vivid, stirring memories. A love for vocabulary would only get stronger with each passing year of school, taught by teachers of the sixties who took sentence structure and penmanship and spelling very seriously.

In my bedroom overlooking maple trees that would turn barn red and gold in autumn, I would pore through dictionaries and newspapers, composing poetry and essays and funny letters to friends. In fifth grade, Miss Alice Helmbrecht told the class that good writing was a skill that would help us all of our lives, no matter what career path we chose. When I learned to type, my love of the craft deepened. At eighty-two words a minute on the keyboard, paragraphs came out in explosive bursts.

Today I think of Miss Helmbrecht when I encourage my Internet-obsessed college classes to spend more time reading great books than sitting in front of their computer screens, lulled by emails and dot-com magazines and other online attractions that are poorly written. I tell them about Oak Park, hometown of Ernest Hemingway, where I grew up reading three thick newspapers: the *Chicago Sun-Times,* the *Chicago Tribune,* and the *Chicago Daily News.*

And I tell those students who are floundering in career directions to think back on what they loved as a child. What a child loves is pure and true. What did you love to do as a child? Are you still doing it, if not full time, at least on the side, like our former baby-sitter Bernice, who has never stopped singing gospel in the church choir, this while working two jobs a day? I was very young when I was first smitten by the crisp language and colorful anecdotes in newspaper stories, and yearned to grow up and be one of those bylines. I wanted a newswoman's life, the most exciting life imaginable—documenting history, dispatching breaking news to the world.

What kids are drawn to initially stems from the soul, a passion that can be molded into a successful and satisfying career. Our preadolescent preferences in work and hobbies often hold the key to what we are meant to do. When we are doing what we were meant to do, we become enmeshed in the creative process, at one with the task at hand, free to fly as high and as far as our imagination. And when our work is fulfilling, stress is reduced and joy is enhanced. And as any good doctor will tell you, a happy heart keeps the body ticking longer.

Helene Anthony used to drive her young son, Chuck, who became my husband, two hours from their home in rural Centreville, Maryland, to the museums of Washington, so he could be inspired to enlarge his passion for drawing and erecting block structures. Today, after years of art lessons and being raised by a mother who repeatedly took him through the magnificent Smithsonian Institution buildings, Chuck has become an architect who loves what he does; design is at the core of who he is.

Oak Park is at the core of who I am, this village of stark seasons and big families and strict teachers and long marriages. I lived in the same house until I went to college, like many Oak Parkers do, and the stability and continuity that dominate life there form the themes of my books. Our boys always make me promise them this about their house on a river in Maryland: "Mom, please, can we live here until we grow up, just like you did in your house in Oak Park?" There is a lot to say for planting deep roots to help create a grounded being; Chuck's family settled in his Maryland hometown on the Corsica River in the 1700s.

Along with giving our own children a home they can count on, I also try to pass on another lesson I learned as a young girl in a community of diverse cultures and income levels: the knowledge that I could be anything I wanted to be, if I stayed focused and worked hard. My father, who grew up poor during the Depression and went on to build a large Chicago-based furniture company called Marvel Metal over the course of forty years, always told me success isn't about luck, it's about sweat and perseverance.

"The harder you work the luckier you will get," was his favorite coaching line. He made me want to keep doing better, and that's about the best a parent can do.

I am dropping my fourth grader Isaac off at school and his teacher, Katherine Haas, raises her arms in a jubilant *V*. "I'm sixty-four today!" she exclaims. The sunlight illuminates her pixie-cut gray hair, and I'm seeing a wide-eyed girl, not a grandmother. As she embarks on the final third of her life, twenty-eight years of it spent teaching third and fourth grade, Haas credits her age-defying exuberance to loving what she does.

"I love, love, love it," says Haas, twirling a red rubber pen with a gaping shark on its top. "I think my family always saw me as the black sheep because my sister has a Ph.D. My brother is a doctor. And I teach nine- and ten-year-olds. But I have always felt I was doing something wonderful. There is always fun in my days.

"I may be sixty-four, but I can still climb trees," Haas adds. "I can't wait to come to school each day and see these little, loving people who have so many questions and keep me thinking. How could anyone spend ten hours a day doing something they don't like to do?"

Here is more from Haas, the daughter of a German mother and a Chinese diplomat father, and a legendary teacher at our children's school, ageless, wild, a Renaissance woman who spends her summers banding loggerhead shrikes and brown thrashers on a Navajo Indian reservation in North Dakota.

Growing up I could not have answered the question: "Who am I?" I wasn't a part of anything. My mother was German and didn't look like me; people thought she was the governess because she had these Chinese-looking babies.

We lived for a while in Germany and in Italy, and no one looked or acted like me. I felt like I never really fit in. I loved drama and dance from the beginning and I started taking ballet and violin and piano lessons. I was good at everything, and I was torn in all these directions. Teaching has brought it all together for me. For a woman who has many interests and talents, teaching is a way of connecting with everything, all at once. I love learning new things from the kids and from other teachers. Right now I'm being tutored in Arabic; I speak three other languages.

When our daughter became an ornithologist, I became her assistant, and now I have become passionate about birds. And I produce the fourth-grade plays. So I never had to give anything up: I get to be part musician, part dancer, part scientist, part mathematician, and very silly or very serious. What other job is like this?

Here I have this very interesting life and my mother was actually ashamed of me because I just have a bachelor's degree. I was always trying to prove to my mom that I'm really an okay person. One afternoon she came to one of my plays at school. People just loved it and walked out complimenting me, and she saw for the first time that I was doing something that wasn't so shameful. I feel very fortunate to be in an environment where everything is always changing and new things are always being introduced. This wonderful puppeteer came to our school, and I told the children, "Oh, wow, maybe that's what I want to be when I grow up!" And one of the kids said, "Mrs. Haas, you are grown up."

Working with children, you always must be awake. They ask marvelous questions, they notice things I miss, and often I have to go home and look up things so I have the answers for them in the morning. So I'm always learning, too. And that keeps me young. I know a lot of people who have lots of degrees and have published a million things, but they have no connection with themselves or with other people. There's no heart, no soul, to their lives. They are successful on paper and successful in other people's eyes, but that doesn't matter. To me, success means I can't wait to come to work in the morning and get right into the hearts of these little people. Success means that I am able to do work that gives me pleasure, a pleasure that helps you grow at every age.

I'm sixty-four and I love birthdays. I never feel like I'm getting old because I'm around children who are so passionate about everything, it just blows me away. And even though I didn't live up to my mother's early expectations, now that she's eighty-nine and she's mellowed, she keeps saying how proud she is of me and how nice it is to have so many children love me. I spent a good part of my life trying to measure up to *her expectations. And it always made me sad that I couldn't, that I was always disappointing her. I was in all kinds of performances, music and dance and violin, and my mother rarely came. And now that I'm directing performances at the school, I love it when the children know their parents are in the audience; it makes all the difference in the world. They are excited, peeking out behind the curtains, trying to find Mom and Dad.*

I have excitement every day. Last week, I told the children Tolstoy's story "The Three Questions." This is about a man who wants to find out how to be a really good person, and he sought the answer to these three questions: When is the best time to do things? Who should I pay attention to and who should I ignore? And what's the very best thing to do? You get to the end and find out that the best time to do things is now. Now is the only time we have any power, not tomorrow. And the best person to pay attention to is who you are with. And the best thing to do is to do good for that person. I told my daughter that ever since I found that Tolstoy story, I'm a different person. And you know what she said that made me feel so happy? "Mom, you're not different. You have always been the most now person I know."

We have all suddenly been forced to reflect on overarching questions about personal happiness, jolted by a black September 2001 and uncertainty over wars without a foreseeable end. At parties and on playgrounds, conversations no longer stall in superficial places. Dialogues now include urgent probes that penetrate right to the heart of the meaning of existence: "Who am I? Who do I want to be? Is it time to quit my job and start living my dreams? What do I want to do with the rest of my life?"

Are you living your dreams? Does going to work fill you with exhilaration, or dread? How can you shift from the grind of the ordinary into the extraordinary? Some sixteen years ago, New Yorker Dick Caples left the law firm of Sherman & Sterling, where he made lots of money as an international banking specialist, to become executive director of the Lar Lubovitch Dance Company. In his new post as director of the nonprofit modern dance troupe, he shifted from a shiny skyscraper and navy suits to jeans and a loft in Chelsea, making half the salary. What Caples told me then about why he turned his life upside down are words that continue to goad and to guide:

"Essentially the practice of law was lacking emotional and psychic satisfaction," said Caples, now fifty-four and still at Lar Lubovitch. "Only in the arts have I been able to feel that my life has greater purpose than merely helping a client make more money. I wanted to be in a job that was touching people in their deepest selves."

Before a metamorphosis can occur, we must first be awakened to our own deepest selves. Then comes the courage to create a life that feels real, passionate, right. And plugging into your passion doesn't have to mean leaving huge earnings behind. The most successful people I know got that way because their fire within and deep-seated self-knowledge has given them an edge to do their jobs better than anyone else. Abbey Butler is a Wall Street legend who grew up in middle-class Brooklyn, where his father managed a variety store. In his second year of college, he started reading the *Wall Street Journal* every day, and "I just knew that was where I belonged," says Butler, sixty-four.

In his first job on Wall Street, running errands at a big investment firm, Butler made $47.50 a week. But what he calls his "real passion and knack" for analyzing stocks and bonds quickly turned into some real money. By the time he was twenty-seven, Butler was a millionaire—this from "devouring more financial news in a week than most people read in a lifetime." The Butler Pavilion and the Norman and Charlotte Butler Learning Institute (named after his parents) at American University are his gifts back to the institution where he studied business, worked to pay his tuition and graduated from in 1958.

"Even when I wasn't making a lot of money, my work has always given me an emotional high," adds Butler, who heads an investment firm called C. B. Equities Corporation. "I have always loved waking up in the morning. I am excited every day. That's what people should strive for. You never want to wake up and say: 'Damn, I have to get up and go to work today.'"

Some of the more interesting twists along Abbey's road to fulfillment and fortune have been to do investment work for various rock groups, such as the Beatles and the Kinks. Walking down the streets of London, Ringo Starr and John

Lennon a few steps ahead of him, in the mid-1960s, Butler recalls exclaiming: "Wow, what a great life I'm having. What I great life I've made for myself."

"After September 11, a lot of people told me they are going after their dreams as quickly as they can," he adds. "It is never too late to start over."

Many of those smitten by the notion of bold forays into more meaningful lives are in their forties, fifties and sixties, no longer shackled by the limits of youth and inexperience. With a good chance that many of the 76 million baby boomers in America could venture beyond their eightieth birthdays, asking the question "Who do I want to be when I grow up?" is no longer something only for kids.

"The old conception is gone that after a certain age it all goes downhill," says Hugh Delehanty, fifty-three, editorial director of AARP Publications and editor-in-chief of *AARP The Magazine.* "With huge advances in medical research, we have not only added twenty years to the average life span, but there is a whole new change in the consciousness of what it means to be alive. People have really opened up to ways they can reinvent themselves at every step.

"When you enter your forties and fifties and get that first glimmer of mortality, many people get released from some of the things that have been holding them back."

In past lives, Delehanty was an editor at both *Sports Illustrated* and *People.* Along the way, he started practicing Zen Buddhism "fairly radically," a journey that led him into a different practice of journalism. In 1995, he coauthored the bestseller *Sacred Hoops* with then–Chicago Bulls coach Phil Jackson, and the following year became the editor of the *Utne Reader,* the nation's leading digest of alternative media.

"I made a decision in my life that I was going to search out work that would integrate where I was evolving as a person," says Delehanty. Joining *Utne* meant moving away from journalism that "celebrated materialism in our culture" to journalism that celebrates basic human values.

"Too many people are prisoners to conceptions of what they are supposed to be," he adds. "Real liberation comes from understanding and following what is happening in your heart."

Nothing slaps us into getting on with our dreams more than hearing that someone middle-aged is sick or dying. I got a call last week from a college friend to say that a friend of ours in her early forties had advanced cancer. The stricken woman, a mother of three young children, had loved hard and lived hard and has always done work she loves. Looking back on her life, she was feeling no major "I should haves" about unexplored terrain. Are there any "I should haves" currently churning in your gut? Becoming the self of your dreams is for right here and right now, not to be posted on some future to-do list that may never pan out.

We all make to-do lists daily and try to do everything on the lists. Recently, I made a to-do life list, and I am determined to accomplish everything on that list as well.

Instead of the usual to-dos, such as "Buy toothpaste" and "Meet Jan at 8:30 for walk," this list has items on it like "Raise $10,000 for The Breast Center," a local breast cancer treatment center, and "Get to know God better." What do you want to accomplish in your life? Put it on paper and get to it. Anything is possible if you have purpose, perseverance, and passion. Those three P words make for an unstoppable person.

Our eight-year-old son Jack recently came bounding into the kitchen, whooping and beaming. He said that he had just discovered that when he was sad he could become happy by just imagining himself smiling. As he put it: "Mommy, I am the president of my imagination, so I can tell myself to be any way I want me to be." With focused imagining, we can all be any self we want to be.

I am in midtown Manhattan having lunch with a man who is one of the biggest names in the publishing world. I ask him who he would want to be if he wasn't who he was. Green eyes flashing, face flushed, this editor in his early forties tells me: "Inside of me is a jazz pianist. And that will happen. You will see."

What will you do for an encore? This is the year to let your fantasies beat out pragmatism and take you where you belong. What are you waiting for? Strike while you are healthy, and have a real shot at re-creation, at truth.

Every morning when I drive the boys to school we cross a bridge and see a 34-foot sailboat docked in Spa Creek in Annapolis. This boat used to bear the name *Forever*

Fifty on its sleek, white body. Recently the name was changed to *Suddenly Sixty*. Those respectable numbers are emblazoned for the world to see, ages that used to be revealed only in embarrassed whispers, especially by women. While their husbands were deemed sexier and more powerful when they hit middle age, turning fifty for females meant a morose passage into menopause. Never again. Wearing Gap jeans and cowboy boots, baby boomers of both sexes blazing through birthdays are shattering any lingering notion that anyone over fifty is on the skids.

As this flashy and loud generation that created the 1960s slogan "Don't Trust Anyone over Thirty" coasts through midlife, aging is no longer an evil to be feared. How could it be, when Gidget, the ever pert and prolific Sally Field, is fifty-six? Reinvention at midlife, a shake-up most of our parents would never have taken on, is our new frontier. Sobered by the Depression and statistics that gave an average life expectancy of about seventy, our parents stayed in one job until retirement, then had only a few happy, golden years to discover passions beyond their jobs. Today, many of those in the first wave of the entrepreneurial baby boom moving toward sixty have their hands in three careers and are training for marathons.

This generation takes the legacy of Thomas Jefferson very seriously, this man who counted the pursuit of happiness as an inalienable right of humankind. So much for fifty being the start of a downward spiral; at midlife, the modern healthy woman can look forward to nearly a third more of her life, outliving her male counterparts by several years. Gail Sheehy's book *New Passages* further documents the revolution in the life cycle. Sheehy calls the feisty midlife stage the Flaming Fifties, promising that women can totally redefine themselves in their forty-fifth year as they propel themselves fully into a second adulthood. So if you're feeling twenty-five and frazzled, don't get winded. It's uphill from here. I tell my college students, who often have lethargy from too much nighttime passion and not enough daytime passion, that I wouldn't turn back the clock for anything. Youth is a time of turmoil and indecision; midlife is a time of celebrating how far you have come and how far you can go. I often feel like I had my midlife crisis at twenty-one; that was the most confusing of times.

"Imagine the day you turn forty-five as the infancy of another life," writes Sheehy. "The stage after forty-five is exciting more and more women to soar into the unknown. As family obligations fade away, many become motivated to stretch their independence, learn new skills, return to school, plunge into new careers, rediscover the creativity and adventurousness of their youths and, at last, listen to their own needs.

"They laugh at themselves for having been so afraid that losing their youthful looks would mean losing their power. On the contrary!"

The heart of today's movement of aging midlifers seemingly growing younger is not about surface detailing. It's about finding your center and having the guts to make your dreams real. It's about feeling like you have more energy than you ever had before. The new middle age means working out at gyms and keeping up with kids young enough to be our kids. I lifted weights in my twenties, stopped for twenty years, then started strength training again a year ago. Four pregnancies have made it so my stomach will never be what it was in college. But now, coached by a patient but relentless trainer, J. D. Adamson, I have muscles in places I've never had them before, and an unprecedented strength to my overall being. After our sessions, I feel the spirit Clarissa Pinkola Estes characterizes in her 1992 bestseller, *Women Who Run with the Wolves*:

"A woman cannot make the culture more aware by saying 'Change,'" she writes. "But she can change her own attitude toward herself.... She does this by taking back her body. By not forsaking the joy of her natural body, by not purchasing the popular illusion that happiness is only bestowed on those of a certain configuration or age, by not waiting or holding back to do anything, and by taking back her real life, and living it full bore, all stops out."

For forty-seven-year-old Moya Keating, "dance has been my identity for as long as I can remember." A professional dancer who quit for a few years to raise her children, Keating is completing a master's degree in dance at New York University's Gallatin School of Individualized Study, and now teaches dance and movement to women through a church workshop. As Keating describes her evolution, it is clear she embodies a woman running with the wolves, someone who reclaimed her real life, with full-bore passion:

My very first memory of myself is when I was about six and we were moving out of our apartment in the Bronx into a split-level house near the beach in Long Island. I remember the open space and bare wood floors and bright sunlight, and I danced and danced on those floors until I slipped and fell on my chin. I still have a mark on my chin from that day.

I began taking dance lessons as a little girl, which felt very confirming, because it was something I loved. Then came the turbulent adolescent years, and dance was my refuge, the place I could calm down. When I was in the sixth grade I had a gym teacher who took us into the city to see Martha Graham, and after I saw Graham perform, I thought, "That's it. That's what I want to do."

At the State University of New York in the mid-1970s, I became a dance major, and I had stumbled into the right place at the right time. My teachers were experimenting in post-modern dance, and the questions they were asking became the questions I would continue to ask throughout my career: "What is dance? What are the limits of dance? Who can be called a dancer?"

After college, I danced professionally for about ten years, in the loft scene of New York City, and in a Houston-based contemporary dance company. Then I got pregnant, and I started thinking: "I'm married. I'm an adult expecting a child. I need to take on adult responsibilities," and even though I had pure love for dance, I left it behind. Then came baby number two.

Immediately I ached to dance. I missed the community of dance, even though with my children I embraced the community of parks and sandboxes for a while. But there was a hole inside of me that wasn't being filled. I felt it very deeply. And I knew there was only one thing that could fill that hole.

About three years into a life of no dance, I surrendered to what was going on inside of me and realized how essential it was to go back to doing what I had so enjoyed as a little girl. And I would dance around the house, just moving, my private little escape. That's how I started again. We moved from Texas to New Jersey and I started to go to ballet classes, and the next thing I knew I found myself again in a small dance company that traveled around the state. I had two children, but I was finding I could do both. I can be passionate about motherhood and still be passionate about dancing.

I remember doing what I call the mommy dance; holding a baby on my hips and rocking back and forth. I always saw things in that way, in movement. Dance is an intuitive connection for me, and even after our third child was born, I was determined not to lose that connection. I knew that I couldn't be the dancer I was when I was twenty. So I had to be willing to constantly reshape my dancing and my image as a dancer, to let it take new form. Now I can't see how I thought it was possible to leave that part of me behind. You cannot leave such an important part of your self.

At the age of forty, I went back to academia to study for a master's degree. It was important for me to remember that dance is the primary method for me to know myself, in ways that are clearer to me than the spoken word. Other people go for long walks in the park to get in touch with themselves. Dance is my way. I must constantly remind myself that this is important work. And that it is important to share.

I've been teaching women of all ages in workshops at a Unitarian church. This is fascinating and challenging work. Because I truly believe that there is a dancer in us all. There are great rewards: students will come to me as if they're telling me a secret; they seek me out, get close to me, and say, "I have to tell you this. I've always wanted to dance." Or they will say, "I danced when I was a little girl and someone told me I didn't have good enough feet." What I do is give them permission to be a dancer, to say: "Yes, I can do this. Yes, I am a dancer." I know what this is like: I have given myself permission to dance. I have said, "Yes, I can do this. I need to do this."

Nondancers often feel uncomfortable at first, there is insecurity. I begin by talking to them about movement. I tell them that we are all moving, all day. I talk about moving around Grand Central Station, where there are no pathways, but people stay out of each other's way, accommodating each other, shaping and moving their body to avoid bumping into somebody, using their peripheral vision and sensing what's around them. And I tell them, "This is dance," and my students just laugh out loud and say, "Oh, good, I know how to do that."

I'm not trying to paint a picture-perfect scene of being in blissful union with my art. There is angst. There are challenges in forming who I will be as a dancer at forty-seven. I'm not making any money at this yet. I envy people who get degrees in nursing and walk out and have a job. I am constantly struggling: Did I make the right choice? Is this important enough to do? But the answer I always come to is yes. Because I followed my passion, it was the right thing to do. It is very inspiring to me to see women in my classes unfold. I tell them they are going to walk in a certain pattern, and the next thing I know they are leaping.

Recently I've been investigating a dance form called Authentic Movement. It's about moving from impulse, very free and expressive. And this form brings me around full circle, to my earliest, authentic self. I always look at that scar on my chin I got when I was six, and that seems very important to me. I think of my body as a road map of myself, and that scar seems almost like a point of departure. It was from there that I was formed. That day is so clear in my mind. I see that light on Long Island near the beach, and leaping across this expansive space in our new house, seeing how I could fill that space, and the bittersweet memory of falling hard enough to give me a scar that I still have.

Now that I am close to fifty years old, I have many, many marks on my body, from childbirth and from years and years of dancing. All those marks seem very precious to me. The dancer grows up with this notion of ideal beauty and youth and the perfect body, and to be dancing with an imperfect body with lots of lines and marks is very exciting.

I dare to be seen in all my midlife glory, with gray hair

and a body that knows gravity telling the story of time. Performing when I was young and had all the prowess of strength and training did not feel risky. Performing now is a jump off the cliff. I hope that, in being seen, I give voice to another kind of strength in a different season of life.

Who Do You Want to Be?

Live Your Dreams, The Time Is Now

It inevitably happens at some juncture in your life, so the time may as well be now: You have a head-on collision with the self you have been dodging, the self you may fear, the self that is defined by your soul and not loved ones' opinions. Stop today, at whatever point you are standing, and confront who you really are—your foibles, your grandeur, your ambiguity about being alone.

Indeed, we all know friends suddenly hit with an empty nest who are waffling in their identity beyond parenthood, or couples holding their marriages together for the sake of the children. We all know men and women who have surrendered their whole selves to lovers, putting all their eggs in one fragile basket. Then the basket of love comes unraveled and they are left bereft, with an unraveled shelf. According to my diaries of college, I was prone to submerging myself in others; self was amorphous, formed around boyfriends and parties. I cringe when I flick through these pages of time. This is from October 1973:

> *I am confused with a Capital C. Will Dave ever call? It's been TWO days. My heart is cracking. He is soooo cute, and makes me feel soooo pretty. I stayed in the dark cave of my bed until 6 p.m. today, too sad to do anything else but wait.*

He did call and we went out for a couple of months. And although he was unreliable, I was too smitten to dump him. That is, until I caught him twice knocking on the door of the girl from Miami down the hall, just after dropping me off in my dorm room. At nineteen, I got my first taste of how awful it feels when someone else holds that much power over you. Yet however hard it was to see Dave and Miss Miami kissing around campus, they gave me the goad I needed to look inside for my power. As I wrote in December 1973:

> *I need to be alone for a period of time, to look only into my own eyes and not constantly seeking others' reflections. I need to leave my friends' lives and find my own. I do not yet know myself; the me I know is mirrored in everybody else. This is not good. I've been protected by parents, adored by friends, and I need to learn how to protect and adore myself. I've been molded by the outside world, and I've never really had to mold myself.*

I must seek my own world. It's time to come to know who I really am. It is scary to become a person.

Although this was written nearly three decades ago, I could have written parts of it yesterday. What's different now is that I have become a person, molded by chance, instincts, determination. I have sought my own world, but it is still scary at times to realize how vulnerable I am, because just when I think I've got the pieces together, something happens to break up the puzzle. After dating some other unreliable men, I married someone totally reliable, which I believe is the sexiest quality you can have in a partner: someone who shows up when he says he's going to show up. Having a partner you can count on gives you a tremendous boost toward coming to love and respect yourself.

Do you have a record of your journey? Pull out your own diaries and look at who you were compared to who you are now. Journals show us our disparate selves—timid and brave, silly and profound. Journals are a road map to our dreams. Since early adolescence, I have documented my most intimate thoughts in books I keep hidden from everybody; they are my secret between me and me. On paper I am at my most honest, my most free.

If you have avoided writing down your soul, it's time to start, no matter how old you are, no matter how busy you are, no matter how wrenching it is to tell the truth. Carl Jung calls these dustballs we've swept under a rug and chosen to ignore, or are unconscious of, the shadow of ourselves. He claims rightly that the "shadow" needs to be integrated into our personalities in order to become whole, or to be, in his terminology, "individuated."

In excavating my own shadows, I see there are core elements that have remained constant with time. I've always wanted to get to the bottom of self. I've always lusted after adventure. I can be supremely confident and supremely insecure. I love to write, and to be surrounded by children. I move too fast. God has a hold on me.

What are the bones of your character? We must know these bones, and build upon them—or else we will be cast adrift from our souls. I know my bones, the brittle ones and the indestructible ones. And while we can metamorphose into thinner people or more muscular people, we can change our religions or wax off body hair, we cannot change our bones. So you gotta love those bones.

My thirty-five years of journal writing remind me that I have often strayed off the track of soul, enticed by strangers who made me forget momentarily who I really am. Yet the path I have followed is basically one paved in truth, and my steps have been guided by instinct and passion. My father used to tell me that people never change, which was important advice when it came to picking a husband. I think my dad was right; no one changes, but over time you stand more revealed as the layers are stripped away. You are who you are, and the quicker you get that, the quicker you get to shed pretenses. When you figure out your truth, you can decide which selves you want to keep, which selves to toss away.

Yesterday I taught a journalism class at American University, where I hold the position of writer in residence, and one young woman student asked me when I first knew I loved to write. I told her about my love affair with language that began with Miss Steger in the first grade. She shook her head and said that at the age of twenty, there was still nothing special she loved to do, other "than going out with my friends."

And I told these students something I have always said to my journalism classes since I started teaching in 1988: Don't leave college without figuring out a cause, a stirring in the heart that feels challenging, inspiring, spiritually right. I told them about the tiny piece of white paper from a fortune cookie I have taped onto my pink iMac computer: "Keep true to the dreams of your youth."

Anything can happen to any one of us at any time. It can happen suddenly and shockingly, when a child gets killed or your doctor gives you a diagnosis of pancreatic cancer. Or it can come on slowly, over years of a thick and gray malaise, one in which you neither hate nor love your life. If you are wallowing in mediocrity, in perpetual questioning: "Is this all there is?" it's time to live the cliché and go get a life. Go get *your* life, the life that no one is holding you back from leading other than you yourself. Set yourself free.

"The Self is freedom!" writes philosopher Søren Kierkegaard. "The more consciousness, the more self; the more consciousness, the more will; the more will, the more self." To me, self as freedom means that becoming a self is an act of will. You take one turn at the fork of the road, and while tugging from spiritual forces and circumstances may cause the needle of the compass to quiver, it is you who chooses to go right or left. Those who surrender to false selves that constrict dreams and desires are destined for ongoing agony. Allow the real blueprint of your self to prevail. You may be able to lie to others during a lifetime, but it is impossible to go a lifetime lying to yourself. Who would want to?

A classic example of a human being whose facade imprisons him is Willy Loman in Arthur Miller's timeless drama *Death of a Salesman*. My first exposure to Loman was as a sophomore in high school, when this saga of a salesman who hates his life inspired me to write a poem on searching for one's true identity that starts off like this:

> *I pondered on a question for what seemed to be a year*
> *The question was quite simple: What am I doing here?*
> *I read and write and talk and walk*
> *But these to no avail*
> *For when I know not why or who it is myself I fail.*

Willy Loman and I met again when the play was assigned in a course called Alienation and Self-Identity, taken while I was studying for my master's degree at Georgetown University. Compared to the best of the world's thinkers who have attempted to decipher the "Who am I and why am I here?" question, Arthur Miller is remarkable at illustrating the plight of a human's search for meaning. Willy is stuck in his role as a mediocre salesman, going nowhere, because he has missed the moment when he could have become his true self, ensconced in nature and his garden, his primal loves.

"Not finding yourself at the age of thirty-four is a disgrace," Willy says to his wife Linda in reference to their son Biff. Willy is overly critical of Biff, a son who yearns for truth of self. Unlike his father, Biff has tried to act out his dreams of living off the land, on a farm, working with his hands. Biff knew the folly of trying to do an office job when in his heart he's an outdoorsman: "Why am I trying to become what I don't want to be?" Biff demands. Willy's son is one up on him; Willy has worked for years, unappreciated, at a job he hates. He doesn't know who he is; he doesn't see who his son really is.

"I don't want a change," Biff snarls at his wife when she tries to slightly alter his routine by surprising him with Swiss cheese rather than the American cheese he always has.

This Arthur Miller classic depicting a sixty-year-old man paralyzed by his own discontent is a universal saga. How many people spend their lives suffocating, drowning? "I realized what a ridiculous lie my whole life has been," Willy laments.

Today, more than half a century after Arthur Miller wrote *Death of a Salesman,* it would be a travesty to live a "ridiculous lie." There has never been a more crucial time to figure out who you are, who you want to be, and how to get to be that person. We must all be unflinching within to steady ourselves against a reverberating world.

Incursions in the Middle East are beamed to us daily by

cable television, the fresh blood splattered on ancient walls, families splintered, hearts torn. As I write this during October of 2002, there is a rupture in the world so deep and widespread that one can't help being shaken and afraid, unsure that anything will ever again be sure and safe. We cling tightly to family or pray urgently to God. But the primary rock we need to lean on is our own selves, and those selves must be our truth.

I remember last spring when my mother called to tell me that a bomb had blown apart a dining room during Passover dinner at a hotel in Natanya, near where our Israeli relatives live. I closed my eyes and took a huge breath, feeling a surge of my own spirit, the throb of my heart, my life within. We must be steadied by the rock of our souls while wars are rocking the planet. As blackness looms, we must be incandescent beings. Every citizen of the earth is suddenly thrust into this reality, even the ones who have never suffered. To not live urgently in these urgent times is a huge mistake. If not now, when?

It is a moment in history when we are all suddenly awake. The circumstances that made our increased state of awareness necessary are horrifying. But to be catapulted into total wakefulness is wonderful, to be wholly alive, to take on a mind set of living each day as if it were our last.

A prominent public relations executive named Luis was diagnosed HIV positive seventeen years ago. Through what he calls his three-track approach, "aggressively treating my emotional, physical, and spiritual sides all at once," Luis remains asymptomatic, a non-progressor, in medical terms—although his intensive drug therapy often causes strong side effects. He spent many years fearful that "the other shoe was going to drop" after his longtime partner died of AIDS. It was only recently that he has let go of the death sentence hovering over his head and started choosing life, as he puts it. Luis is newly in love and the couple just bought a house with a backyard for their Lhasa apso; he is planning a trip to Europe and saving money for retirement.

Handsome and ruddy in a white Italian shirt and an olive jacquard tie, Luis, forty-three, illustrates for all of us the importance of packing life in every hour of every day.

I was diagnosed in June of 1985. When I was told, I thought, "I'm twenty-six, and my God, I'm going to die." AIDS at this time was completely uncharted territory, and all we knew about it was that it was a fatal disease and there was no cure. Gay men were dropping like flies. But as time went on and I looked over the landscape, there were people out there living with AIDS, not dying. And I knew in my heart, I just knew with every fiber, that there had to be a multi-faceted approach to what they were doing and I had to figure it out. That if I lined up ten of these long-term survivors, they may all be totally different, but there was common ground between them, and I had to identify what the common ground was beyond AZT, which was the only drug for a very long time. And for me, it turned out to be a three-track combination of emotional, physical and spiritual components.

And this, with a lot of luck, is why I'm alive after seventeen years, and every June I celebrate as if it is my birthday. My first lover died of AIDS within four years after he was diagnosed, and he did not have the level of emotional or spiritual support that I have in my life, and who knows? Perhaps that would have prolonged his life. When he died in 1986, there were also no sophisticated drug cocktails that are available to us now. But I have always had a strong support structure. I've been in the same job for my entire adult life. It is challenging, interesting work, and my immediate boss knows everything about me and this illness and is behind me completely.

I work myself silly, both because the job calls for it but also because I love what I do. I've got superb friends, parents and siblings who love me, and I'm active in the Episcopal Church. God, I believe, has had an enormous role in keeping me around. And I am aggressive in working with my doctors and in bringing other nontraditional remedies into their standard mix of medicine. I don't hold on to anything that isn't working. For example, I tried vitamin C therapy for a couple of years and that didn't work. Then I stopped sugar for a while because I felt intuitively that's what I needed to do. It's a constant balancing act, and I know how many balls I have to keep up in the air at one time because if I drop the wrong ones, the end could begin.

For about fifteen years after the diagnosis, I was waiting for the other shoe to drop. Now that it's been seventeen years, I live more presently, and I do allow myself to plan for the future. I'm in a new relationship, and we just bought a house together and I plan to spend the rest of my life with him. But I'm not going to fool myself into thinking everything is okay;

this illness is always on my radar screen. I've had periods since 1985 where I've thought of the HIV nearly every minute of the day. In this period of my life, I do not, although I do take handfuls of pills every day, so it is a constant reminder.

There is always tension between being realistic and being hopeful. You know, after September 11, when Tom Ridge and John Ashcroft keep putting the country in a heightened state of alertness for terror, I realize that this is how I live my life every single day. I am always in a heightened state of alertness. For seventeen years, terror has been lurking right around the corner. I awake each day not sure if my personal sleeper cells will become activated. And it has made me a more urgent, focused person. Anyone who knows me well would describe me as someone who lives full tilt, a risk taker.

I know this sounds strange, but if someone said, "I'll grant you any three wishes you want, anything in the world," I would not wish away my HIV. I mean, who wouldn't wish for world peace? Who wouldn't wish to abolish poverty? But I'm talking about personally, I wouldn't wish to be a different Luis. Because no one has guaranteed longevity, and I may live longer than many perfectly healthy people you know. Or I may get mowed down in the street tomorrow.

HIV has given me a clear purpose for being here, and I am grateful for that. Most people are reluctant to face certain things about themselves. With me, I cannot avoid them, because deep questions about who I am and mortality visit me and revisit me constantly. I am transformed in ways that I never would have never been transformed. There is a perpetual gratefulness for the people who love me and who have stood by me. And I am grateful to God for my being led to this place. In spite of the power of the HIV virus within me, God is in me, too. My doctors count my viral load, and right now they are nearly undetectable. They have been up to a million in previous years. What I count on is the voice within that tells me that the presence of God is the very form and substance of every cell in my body. When I become afraid, I try to remember that God is closer to me than my own breath. It is a never-ending source of love and of light.

I am more humbled by the HIV than I am afraid of it. There's almost an electricity about it, not like an ego-powering of "I can do anything." It's more like "How can I stay true to myself every step?" There are no right answers on how to lead one's life, but I know that every choice I have made, I have been true to myself. I have confronted myself in ways very different from most people I know. I understand the randomness of life. I understand the power of today. I understand the power of God. When anybody has this diagnosis, you are challenged to travel to places most people don't want to go. But I have the freedom to tackle my primal fears, like death, which most people don't want to talk about or think about, but is something that is certainly present for me all the time.

I used to turn to God all the time and say, "I want the answers." And the answer to me, over the period of seventeen years, is that there are no answers but to live my life with grace and gratitude. I feel that this attitude has helped my body be more resilient. And love has had a lot to do with the answer on why I got to this place where I am now. I haven't seen my therapist for a while, but I went recently for my annual checkup.

And I said to him, "How could this be happening? I'm not just surviving, I'm thriving." I am not destroyed, I am stronger than ever. And sometimes I just don't get it. But I do get that it's not just about taking pills on schedule. It's not just about being in love. It's not just about the spiritual peace. It's a lot about being willing to honor the voice of my true self and to be flexible.

When AIDS was first diagnosed, I was told that the onset of this illness from the point of HIV infection was three to five years. And I said, "Okay, I can get there." Then, with new treatments, they pushed it back to seven years. And I said, "I can get there." Then it was nine years, and I got there, and eleven years, and I got there, and thirteen years, and I got there, and now I know very few people who are living longer than me. I feel like I live under a net and the boundaries of the net keep shifting, expanding, and I have to keep shifting and expanding. I don't buy into the hope that there is a miracle out there. But I do buy into the idea, for the first time in seventeen years, that I do have a future and I am planning for it in ways that I never planned before.

While I've never had an opportunistic infection, this journey has not been without problems. I have to keep changing my medicines, because every couple of years the ones I'm taking stop working, and I've gone through just about everything. I've been on something for two years now that is working but has very powerful side effects, and I know that this drug, too, will run its course. But for right now, it is what it is and I'm OK with change and adapting. I've done it many times before.

You know, I didn't plan on living this long, and once it really hit me, I thought, "Well, now what am I going to do?" I *started an IRA. I am saving money in the bank. I can imagine being seventy and retired. For the first fifteen years, it was always in my mind: "Oh, I'm going to die from this." I'm no longer constantly thinking death. And that feels good.*

I just wouldn't wish any of this away. I would not give this up for anything. I live in a constant state of extreme gratefulness, and how many people can claim that? This disease has made it so that I wake up every day saying thank you, and I am determined to fill my time with as much love and adventure as possible. One of the reasons I'm still here is that I believe I still have work to do. Another reason I'm here is that there's not any part of my life that I edit from anybody. My friends and my family see me in truth, I live in truth, and I love in truth and am loved in truth. And whether gay or not, if you are hiding yourself, your issues, your pain, that takes a huge toll on your health. My partner who died, he had to edit himself all the time. He was isolated, he didn't have the close family relationships, he lacked a strong social network. Did he die so quickly because he had to keep so much of himself away from other people? You cannot keep something like this inside of you. It's like an ulcer eating at your soul.

I often ask myself, What is God's role in this? I was raised Catholic, but I don't buy into the view that every minute of my day is mapped out by God. I have free will, and free choice, and that's a big part of why I'm alive. God's part is in making me see that by becoming broken I have become whole in a way that most people will never experience. I was in a government building on September 11. We were ordered to evacuate, to drop everything and run right after the Pentagon was hit. My first thought was this is my dumb luck. I've sur-vived AIDS for seventeen years and now I'm going to die because of this. What I came out of September 11 thinking is that we can all create these illusions that "I'm safe" or "I'm healthy," but there really aren't any guarantees. Any of us could go at any time. None of us should ever be fooled into thinking "Well, nothing could touch me." Everything can touch you. You can get sick or your child could get kidnapped or your building could be hit by a plane.

I'm very clear that HIV is a gift. And I know that it sounds bizarre, but it is absolutely a gift that changed my life, and jolted me into finding out who I am.

You know, we're all broken, we're all imperfect, so I don't feel that different than anyone else. But we don't all accept our brokenness, and I do. I am reminded that I am broken every day, and I embrace the pieces of that self. I know those pieces very well, and over the last couple of years they are fitting together very well. My partner has a house on the Atlantic Ocean and we spend a lot of time there during the summer. I love to body-surf, and the energy I get by being on that wave, not trying to control my movement, but just riding with the current. I get pulled under if I don't navigate right. To me, that captures everything about my life, because sometimes I get all the way to shore and other times I get pulled under, but every moment is intense. I'm very energized by it. And when I do get swallowed by a wave, I jump right back in. I don't even dust the clumps of sand off my body.

And that's my life. I get battered, bashed around, some-times pulled under, sometimes I ride all the way to the shore, but I always get back into the water. And here I am today: I'm still standing. I've lost about fourteen close friends to AIDS. And it's a little lonely on this end. I do ask myself often: What the hell am I doing right? The other part of me goes: Don't get complacent, ever. There is no safety zone for you.

My advice to other long-term survivors is to build a dream in your mind of where you want to go, and you can get there. I'm a great planner and organizer, and I always have something on my calendar I can look forward to. And I get there. This gives me a focus, it gives me hope, it gives me purpose, it gives me a reason. You know, the alternative is flailing around on a couch, saying "Woe is me." I choose to embrace this day.

I'm resistant to more drugs than I care to admit to. So if they don't develop some stuff in a hurry and this current treatment fails, I could start to slide off the corner of the curb. But that's not where I'm ready to be. And I am with a partner who has an attitude of whatever happens will happen, and he is in this moment with me. I ask sometimes: How can I bring somebody into a relationship that could be as tough, unfair, and devastating as what I went through when my first lover died? But what is driving me to have a full life, a life of love, is this feeling I have to keep getting back up on that wave until I'm too old or too tired to surf. I'm running at 100 percent of who I am. There is no safety for any of us that tomorrow is coming, so let's do it now. Something could happen to my partner before it happens to me. As hard as it is to imagine, I know that I would pick myself up again.

I feel unencumbered. I feel less stress by virtue of the fact that my life is real. I have refused to allow my psyche to be destroyed by all the talk of AIDS being only about fatality and death. If I got those three wishes and I wished to be healthier, would that guarantee that I would have more joy in my life? No. I used to watch Let's Make a Deal *with Monty Hall, it was one of my favorite shows, where you would trade in cash and you could win a Mercedes or a 1950s clunker. What if I traded this in and I got a worse clunker? I'll take what I've got. This is who I am and I'm okay with that. I'm too happy with this journey.*

Are you okay with who you are? I'm getting there, inspired by Luis, who has become a dear friend, a lamp lighting my path. He reminds me in minute and monumental ways that I will never know the breadth of my reach if I am afraid. I was at the Atlantic shore with my family recently, thinking of Luis wiping out in the choppy waters, without dusting the sand off his body, and flinging himself back out in the surf. I love swimming in the waves, but once I get decked, I usually retreat to my beach chair, soggy and defeated, and call it a day. No more.

With Luis on my mind, I started going back for more after bad falls, to ride the next wave, which was always a bigger and better blast, a high I would have missed if I had given up. Giving up eliminates the fun, and in Luis's case, not giving up has meant the difference between life and death. His dream was to live as normal and long a life as possible, and he rolled up his sleeves and went to work on achieving that dream. This is a man who prays regularly to

God, but he knows that God needs help to make our dreams come true.

Of course, dreams must be realistic, within reach. You can't be fifty-three and become twenty-three. But you can be forty-one and get a pilot's license, after a life spent fantasizing about being in the driver's seat of an airplane.

Software executive Wesley Jones, forty-four, has wanted to be a pilot ever since he was a small child who collected model airplanes and books on aviation. Jones's father died when he was thirteen, and he shelved his dreams, instead bouncing around odd jobs after high school before going to college to study computer science. Driven by both the need to make money and a fire within, Jones joined Ciena and helped build it into the world's leading corporation in fiber-optic transport and switching systems. When he took a buyout four years ago, the self-made multimillionaire had plenty of time on his hands to revive old dreams. He took his first flying lessons in March 1999 and got his private pilot's license the following year. He has since started a new software company, Live Capsule, but has vowed never to get so swamped by work that he doesn't have time to fly.

I read about him in the local newspaper last Memorial Day weekend. He and his flight instructor survived a crash in their single-engine Commander by ditching the aircraft, which had fallen into the South River, and quickly surfacing. I ran into Jones three days after the accident and asked him how he was. He told me he was fine. In fact, he was taking an aerobatics stunt lesson later that day. Here's why a man who nearly lost his life in an airplane says he will never stop flying:

SURRENDERING TO YOURSELF

You can't imagine the spiritual high of looking down on the clouds from a small plane, on top of a sea of billowy marshmallows. The freedom of flying your own plane is like nothing you ever feel on a commercial airliner. If I want to turn around and fly into the sun for a while, or if I want to take a better look at that mountain over there, I do what I want to do when I want to do it.

A couple of weeks ago, two friends and I took off from Baltimore in my little airplane, a Commander single-engine four-seater, and went to Lake Tahoe. We took two days and hopped our way across the country, across the incredible lush greenery of the Midwest, across the barren wastelands beyond Kansas, across the Rockies, across the desert, and finally to the Sierra Nevada mountains. The entire country just rolled by under the wings.

Flying at the altitudes I fly at, between 6,000 and 12,000 feet, you can see farmers working in their fields, you can even identify crops. We flew over over some of our country's most beautiful sights—Mount Rushmore, Arches and Canyonlands National Park, and Lake Powell in Utah; we zigzagged our way across the Grand Canyon for more than an hour, back and forth. And when we got to Lake Tahoe in the late afternoon, the sun was setting over the Sierra Nevada mountains and it looked like a pool of liquid gold.

Never once did it cross my mind to stop flying after our plane crashed. I will never give this up, but I will never forget that day. I was out with my instructor, coming back from an aerobatic lesson, when the engine quit in our plane. We had just enough time to run through the emergency checklist while

· 69 ·

looking for a clear spot to land. The only suitable place clear of people, homes, and trees was the river.

The plane submerged, and we immediately popped the canopy off the plane, and in zero visibility—murky, muddy water—we had to unhook our five-point seat-belt harness, get out of our parachutes because they were jamming us into the plane, and swim out underneath the inverted aircraft. The whole ordeal took about one minute. We were still sinking while we were swimming out; the plane had not yet hit the bottom.

The first thought I had was that I had survived. We were actually spared any injury at all because in an aerobatic plane, like a race car, you are strapped in very tightly, so you aren't jostled on impact like you would be in a regular plane. And I kept thinking that I'm going to keep my cool and just do what I have to do, feel around these seat-belt buckles in thick brown water, from silt stirred up when the plane went down. And I calmly thought that I just have to hold my breath as long as it takes. We both got out cleanly with only minor cuts and scrapes to show for it.

I was back up in my plane two days later. It was important to get back up as quickly as possible, because your most recent memories are your most powerful. I didn't want to have any fear of flying. Flying is a dream come true.

All my life I've wanted to be a pilot. When I was nine, I used to put together model airplanes. I literally had dozens and dozens of them. I would spend hours and hours studying diagrams of planes, reading books on planes and pilots. If I had some encouragement from my parents or a guidance counselor in high school, I probably would have joined the Air Force or the Navy and trained to be a pilot.

My dad died the week before I turned fourteen. I had a younger brother and sister and my mom had to work two jobs, and I ended up sort of wandering after high school. Instead of going right to college, I took about two years and raced motor-cycles and drank too much beer and worked odd jobs, but then I had an epiphany that really changed my life.

When I was twenty, I was working in a Sears outlet store, cleaning up returned refrigerators and appliances and putting them back on the floor for resale. This is what I was doing while all my good friends were in college. One day I was sitting there in the warehouse with the other guys. They were in their forties and fifties, and this was the only job they'd ever had, this is all they'd ever done. And here I am, a twenty-year-old, having my sandwich in the warehouse with these middle-aged guys who were going nowhere. And basically I realized this is all I'm ever going to be if I don't pull myself up and get it together. Everybody my age I knew was out there studying, making themselves into something more. And here I was just barely being something, and that something didn't make me very happy.

I sat there in that warehouse that day and cried. The very next day I applied to college, got accepted the next quarter, and became the biggest overachiever in the computer science department that college has ever seen. I think this fire in my belly didn't come from anyone else. I gave it to myself. Ever since my dad died, I had been waiting for someone else to guide me, and I came to the realization that no one else was going to do that. I had to do it myself. That afternoon at Sears I took charge of my life, and I just never looked back.

I finished my education, and over the next eighteen years worked in the early development stage of four successive high technology start-ups while raising a family. I was way too busy to pursue my dream of flying, but it was always there in the back of my mind. From time to time, a friend or coworker would talk about learning to fly and I'd think, "If I only had the time and money finally to do that." But I think I unconsciously knew that if I ever started flying, it would consume me totally. And it just wasn't the right time to take my eye off the ball of creating wealth for my family.

Flying on the side really puts my business life into perspective. When we're out trying to raise money for our highly speculative start-up company Live Capsule in a bad economy, no matter how tough it gets, it's not like crashing into a river. It's not like your life is going to be over if this company doesn't get funding or if the customer says no. My business is no longer the thing that validates who I am; I probably define myself more as a pilot than a software entrepreneur. Because flying is my primary passion, it's who I am. If anything in your life can ever mean as much to you as your family, a core passion, then flying is right up there.

What unfinished business from childhood do you have gnawing at your soul? It's time to become who you wanted to be when you grow up, even if you're already fifty-four years old. Everyone needs some joy beyond their day job, some recreation in which to re-create self, some mystery.

One of the world's greatest creators, Albert Einstein, had this to say on the subject: "The most beautiful thing we can experience is the mysterious. . . . He to whom this emotion is a stranger, who can no longer pause to wonder and stand rapt in awe, is as good as dead; his eyes are closed."

Figuring out what is missing from a life with no rapture can be as simple as taking a yellow legal pad, drawing a line down the center, and making two lists: "What I love about my life," and "What I hate about my life." Then root around in your psyche and come up with a wish list. Much of what you want is achievable.

Some of my best decisions have been made by simply weighing up pros and cons, then taking action. I left daily journalism because it was eating the heart out of my family life, and we moved from Washington, D.C., to a riverfront community an hour away so our children could grow up with space around them, on the water, among a more earthy, less transient population. In my former life, I had become a mechanical being, sprung and overwrought, breathlessly sprinting with no time for reflection. Like Wesley Jones, my early passions were buried in an adrenaline-charged career. I had a great job but no time, and living in the city often felt like living in a cage.

In 1994, when we first saw what would become our new house, we fell instantly in love with its weathered shingles, which make it look like a camp lodge, and its location on the crest of a hill. Seeing two lizards scurrying across the back stone steps and a fawn near the red barn clinched the deal. I have always been the happiest in the country, and so has my husband. We are home here.

Where do you belong? Is the place you live in a house but not home? Is your job eating the heart out of your family life? However risky and frightening it is to uproot if it means saving your soul, it must be done. Years ago while I was at UPI, there was a coterie of veterans of the wire service in their fifties and sixties, cigarettes dangling from their mouths. They had worked half their lives there in front of their typewriters, which turned into computer terminals in the early 1980s. These grizzled reporters were mesmerizing characters, with their stories from the front lines of civil rights marches led by Martin Luther King, of battles in Vietnam, of the day Richard Nixon resigned.

But away from the newsroom and the pulse of the moment, many of these reporters drank too much, were plagued by poor health and had failed marriages. Daily journalism is more interesting than almost any other field, but there is no even ground; you are constantly fluctuating between the highs of hammering out stories on deadline and spiraling downward, until the next high comes around. After seven years in the business, too high, too low, beaten, I bailed. It was an exhilarating ride, but felt more like an addiction than a life.

I recently had lunch with a television producer friend and we were talking about the catch-22 of being a journalist in Washington: there is no more exciting city to be a reporter in, but news breaking every minute can break you as a person. He told me about an old friend of his, Bob Currie, who left his spot at the pinnacle of national journalism, as an investigative producer of ABC's *Primetime Live,* after a thirty-seven-year climb through all of the major networks to get there.

In 1991, Currie and his wife and nine-year-old son moved to Wimberley, Texas—Hill Country, where LBJ is from. I called Currie and found him on his back deck, looking out into the Blanco River Valley and the lush Paradise Hills in the distance, turning gold as the sun went down. Here is his tale of leaving the journalism capital of the world for a town near Austin where he knew no one, and that has one Dairy Queen but no McDonald's.

At one time, I was executive producer of the CNN investigative unit and had done some stories down in Texas. I found this place we now live in the Hill Country, in the center of the state, and I was just fascinated by it. My wife, Salwa Khan, was the video editor for MacNeil-Lehrer, yet we both have a back-to the earth mentality.

We were living in Silver Spring, Maryland, our son was four, and we decided that by the time he was nine we would not be living in the Washington area. We made some trips back to Texas, and my job at ABC was not going well, and I felt like nothing bound me to the East Coast anymore. I'm originally from North Carolina, and Washington never felt like a real place; it's an artificial construct caught in a crack between Maryland and Virginia. People think it's so beautiful on Capitol Hill, but it's an unreal beauty. You drive five minutes and Washington becomes a poor and ugly place, a real place.

Washington didn't warm my soul. I wasn't a politician. I started out being an artist; my college degree is in art history. And I always wanted to somehow go back to a more artistic life. I never felt like I was meant to be in Washington. It wasn't my life; being a reporter is telling about someone else's life, what somebody else did. I felt like I wanted to do some of my own things, to paint and draw again. I do computer-enhanced drawings and paintings, and I have had some exhibitions since we've been in Texas.

We moved from a house outside Washington where you could throw a rock and hit the Beltway to a log house on two acres, where it's hard to see your neighbors. This town had a population of about 5,000 when we moved here. We didn't know anyone in Wimberley, but we came with open minds and the people here are real friendly. We left with no jobs waiting for us in Texas. Salwa and I started a production company, vcYes Productions, and we do video and multimedia projects. We are not getting rich, and that's fine, really. We love it here.

You get to a point in your life, and you go, "Why not? What's holding me back?" My wife and I chose to find a sanctuary where we could bring up our boy and have him grow up like I grew up in the hills of North Carolina. There was nothing stopping us. We had lived a life up to that point of being careful, trying to do the right thing, trying to do the smart thing in terms of our careers. And I was thinking, "I can't do this for the rest of my life."

Completely starting over again has helped me stay young, rather than becoming a fossil journalist like I would have in Washington. I'm doing things now that I've never done before, like learning about computers and the Internet. I'm fifty-six, and I think I have aged pretty well. I've worn maybe two suits since I've been here, both times to funerals. My uniform here is casual slacks, T-shirts, sandals. Now that I'm here, I don't know how people live any other way.

When I was coming up in North Carolina, everything was so real to me. Everybody worked in tobacco, many of them had dirty hands, and everybody in Wimberley feels so real too. Here most of the people I know built their own houses with their hands. They keep their own horses and ride them every day. They grow their own food. We have our own garden here with all sorts of things in it—beets, lettuce, cabbages, corn, tomatoes.

Fear keeps people in place, and I didn't have that fear. Now that we are empty nesters—our son is an officer in the U.S. Navy—I've got more time to appreciate what a fantastic person my wife is. Evenings, at sundown, we can watch Paradise Hills across the way turn various shades of gold and green.

RESURRECTING CHILDHOOD JOY

What is the passion of your soul? Do you know? Have you lost your raw child energy? We cannot all build careers around passion, such as many artists are able to do, but we can all stay connected to that early joy. I love riding horses, and I rode often until I was in my mid-twenties. Throughout my life, I dreamed of owning a horse ranch in Tucson, Arizona, where my family vacationed throughout

IRIS KRASNOW

my childhood, and where my brother Greg now lives.
Whether that ever happens—and I still hold on to the
hope that it will—I can still ride horses in my home state
of Maryland. I can still live part of my dream.

I recently got on a horse again after a two-decade break,
at my friend Marian Shaw's 190-acre farm off the Chester
River in eastern Maryland. As she was adjusting my stirrups
on a mare named Iris, of all names, I put my head on the
horse's red mane, stroked her sinewy neck and the smell of
sweat and hay shot me back to my horse Chico from girlhood and the tobacco-chewing cowboys who led us on trails
through the Arizona desert. Cowboy Frank is an indelible
memory. He wore tight jeans and smoked Camel non-filters
and he made the best scrambled eggs fried in bacon grease
on breakfast rides—this while drinking a Coors beer from
the can.

With tears streaming through the dust on my cheeks, I
took off with Marian next to fields of soybeans and new
emerald green wheat. Everything good and right about riding came rushing back to me: loping against the wind, my
muscles molded onto the horse's muscles, moving as one,
like a sexy slow dance. As we eased to a halt, I let a hot and
glisteny Iris chomp on some bushes, then put my hands on
the horn of the Western saddle and threw my head back.
Under a blinding October sun and surging with history, my
whole self opened.

How could I have left horses, the sport of my soul? I
ride as often as I can these days and will never stop. That
was a huge mistake.

What are you hankering to do that you stopped doing? As parents we are delegated to the sidelines, to watch as our children exalt in tackling new sports and activities. While we are proud audience members as they learn to horseback-ride, score goals in soccer, excel at ballet and get up on water skis, all this can make us want to dig in ourselves. Pushing ourselves to get off the observation deck and back into the game can make anyone feel giddy, like a grown-up who is still growing, not someone edging over the hill. Grab your old skateboard or guitar, pick up on writing the novel you started in college, go back to something you once loved but left. You too will feel as if you've unlocked a precious piece of yourself that got buried with time and responsibility.

I bought a copy of Norman Vincent Peale's *The Power of Positive Thinking* for two dollars at a used-book store, curious about this half-century-old bestseller and its author, the patriarch of the self-help movement. His methods for showing readers that you must not be defeated by anything are centered around letting Jesus Christ take control and therefore may not seem accessible to non-Christians. Yet beyond his simplistic solutions for praying your troubles away there is real power to be gotten from some of Peale's pages, such as this memorable passage I have copied and sent to friends:

> *A famous trapeze artist was instructing his students how to perform on the high trapeze bar. Finally, having given full explanations and instruction in this skill, he told them to demonstrate their*

ability. One student, looking up at the insecure perch upon which he must perform, was suddenly filled with fear. He froze completely. He had a terrifying vision of himself falling to the ground. He couldn't move a muscle, so deep was his fright. "I can't do it! I can't do it!" he gasped.

The instructor put his arm around the boy's shoulder and said, "Son, you can do it, and I will tell you how. . . . Throw your heart over the bar and your body will follow. Fire the heart with where you want to go and what you want to be. In other words, throw the spiritual essence of you over the bar and your material self will follow."

"Throw your heart over the bar and your body will follow" comes down to knowing: "I am, therefore I can." What fears do you hold that are blocking you from soaring over high bars? Pushing yourself over high bars, even if it's just for a couple of hours a week, separates those who are merely existing from those who are staying alive, writhing with life.

My husband, Chuck, has started playing basketball with a group of middle-aged men, all hoop stars in high school and college, every Sunday morning. Hesitant at first to start again after years away from the game, Chuck now charges out of the house, as excited as I've ever seen him. Playing two hours of basketball for a forty-six-year-old architect who sits behind a desk all week is far beyond an excellent cardiac workout; this newfound pastime drawn from an old-time passion exercises his whole being.

Californian Coburn Haskell, an accountant, was the bass player in the top rock band at Stanford University while we were there in the 1970s. After a very long hiatus, two years ago Haskell, now fifty, started playing rock music in the Rockinghams, a local rockabilly band made up of middle-aged men from Los Angeles. Here's what it feels like to be performing on stage again, holding his old Fender bass guitar:

Playing in a rock 'n' roll band on the side has to be the dream of every aging rock and roller turned blue/white-collar wage earner, longing for the camaraderie, creativity, and cheap thrills of a bygone time. Performing in public for the first time in 17 years triggered that glorious combination of Jell-O-knees anxiety and breathtaking exhilaration. However, the purest joy this time around comes not from the ego-enhancing adulation of strangers partying to a band with a combined 125 years of rock 'n' roll musicianship under its size thirty-four to thirty-six belts. The real rush came when the band—the guys—really locked into the groove, or "the pocket," as musicians call it; when the music suddenly takes on a life of its own and transcends to a higher timeless plane, taking the boys in the band along for a joy ride where all barriers to musical communication and shared expression have suddenly, magically, dissipated. That's the real thrill.

Remember who you are, no matter what your day job is. We all need to stay linked to our inner source of raw, animal energy. Raw energy means you are putting your soul work on canvas or into a garden or onto a basketball court.

Raw energy is creativity, and enmeshed in the creative process, humans are their happiest, their most soulful. You know the expression "He's a lost soul." What this translates to is that his soul is there, and he is there, but the two are separated and need to be reunited. That union can be accomplished by regularly coming out from under an oppressive day job.

Ben Michaelson has a bustling real estate law practice by day; at dusk he changes out of his suit into jeans and moves into his backyard to tend his bonsai, miniature trees that require painstaking discipline, patience, and skill. Overlooking woods and a river, Michaelson digs in the dirt and lovingly attends to forty tiny trees, apart from clients who want a piece of him and telephones that never stop. Here is what it feels like to sink your fingers into a passion apart from the grind:

My passion for bonsai began a number of years ago when visiting a friend who was baby-sitting a tree for a neighbor. I was struck by the beauty of the "tree in a pot"—the literal translation of the word bonsai.

Working with bonsai provides me with a way to totally remove myself from the everyday stresses of life. I relax when immersed in the creation of works of natural beauty. One must look at a tree for what it is to become, not just when you are finished working on it today, but for what you want it to look like years from now.

Once created, a bonsai tree becomes like a child. It needs to be properly fed, watered, and changed, or repotted period-

ically. As with a child, it requires daily attention, discipline, and lots of tender loving care. And like a child, if it is given the proper amount of care and attention, the end result is most gratifying.

I lost one of my trees in the recent drought when the sprinkler system malfunctioned while I was on vacation. I was so upset when I discovered what had happened that I punched the wall and chipped a bone in the back of my hand. It was as though I had lost one of my best friends. This was a tree that I had trained from nursery stock and had nurtured for the past twelve years. My frequently aching hand reminds me that I probably take my hobby too seriously sometimes.

Don't forget to keep your own spirit flowing by spending at least a fraction of every day connecting with tasks that tweak your soul, even if that means an occasional explosion of emotion. Better to let it out than bubble inside with discontent.

I did a long profile of artist Robert Rauschenberg for United Press International in 1985, after spending a day with him in his studio north of Houston Street in New York City. Sipping from a tumbler of Scotch, he talked a lot about the spirit behind his collages made of slathered paint and pieces of junk that first appeared at the Betty Parsons Gallery in 1951. Rauschenberg, who is jointly credited with Jasper Johns as an iconoclast who opened up the vein of Abstract Expressionism that led to Pop Art, spoke of a "wild energy that is really gorgeous."

"I feel like my whole life is like a pile of mud, and it's only good if you sling it." Rauschenberg smirked, reminding me that my own life at the time felt like mud, or perhaps quicksand; I certainly felt stuck. I was addicted to my job interviewing famous people but starting to feel rumblings of discontent, a sense that in my late twenties, I needed to sling myself in a new direction, back to earth, out of the clouds. And when I left Rauschenberg I did end up moving into a new self. I met Chuck soon after, and dating him gave me good reason to loosen the tyranny of my career, which allowed the wife-mother self to surface. Rauschenberg, the artist who made his name mixing up Coke bottles, chains, feathers, clock faces and stuffed chickens with paint, explained that the trick to maintaining wild energy is to keep mixing up your life: "One of my basic criteria is that once I feel secure in a technique or an attitude or an idea or a material, I have to change, because the adventure is gone. It's terrible if you hang on just a few minutes too long."

Some people hang on not just a few minutes, but a few decades too long, losing the moment to revive a life resonant with wild energy, energy to sling and hurl and transform.

Raw energy is abundant in our youth, when lazy afternoons are spent with crayons and construction paper. Children get absorbed in the creative process, coloring pictures that come straight from their soul. I think of Picasso's great line: "It took me an entire life to learn how to draw like a child." Don't lose your entire life before you resurrect the pure passions you had when you were young. Acting on childhood passions is how greatness happens.

Albert Schweitzer, the grand thinker and healer, also possessed a formidable talent for the piano. He came from a long line of organists and was enchanted by music from early childhood. When Schweitzer first heard a duet sing the lyrics "In the Mill by the Stream," he was so dizzy with excitement he had to prop himself against a wall. "The charm of the two-part harmony of the song thrilled me all over, to my very marrow," he wrote in *Memoirs of Childhood and Youth*. "And similarly the first time I heard brass instruments playing together I almost fainted from excess of pleasure."

When he went to work as a doctor in Africa during World War I, he took his piano with him. In the quiet of the night, after long days tending to villagers stricken with tuberculosis and malaria and other tribal scourges, Schweitzer's music could be heard in the equatorial forest, on the banks of the Ogowe River. Playing piano was his poetry, his balm for the soul, fortifying his capacity to apply healing hands to others.

Remember who you are. It's not only about staying linked to old hobbies; it's also about remaining linked to old friends.

This morning I called my friend Terry Rubin in Denver, a woman I've known since 1966, when we were ten and in Cabin 6 at Camp Agawak in Minocqua, Wisconsin. We were both on the Blue Team and both had the same sense of daring and humor. We were best friends summer after summer, and then in our teens, we stopped going to camp. We talk several times a year, and when I hear her voice I scream and laugh like I did at ten. She has that effect on me, an instantaneous joy that wells in a place that only Terry knows. Terry is the only friend I have who remembers getting Slow Poke caramel suckers stuck in our braces.

Simone Gould, a friend since freshman year in college, is another soul sister until the end. When the weather was irresistibly inviting and the prospect of being penned up with professors seemed too grim, we would ditch class, slather on baby oil, get into bikinis, tin-foil our Rod Stewart album covers, stick our chins in the fold, and fry to a golden brown. We still hoot until we cry over our purchase of a 1961 white station wagon for $150, a rusted Plymouth with torn blue plastic seats we named Abraxas, in honor of the Carlos Santana album. The only way Abraxas would start was if one of us turned on the ignition and pumped the gas pedal while the other got under the hood and jiggled the battery cable. Abraxas lived for four fantastic months, shuttling us all over, from mountainside taverns outside of Boulder, Colorado, to a Santana concert in San Francisco.

Miles away from my cluster of ancient sisters, I seek in new friends the spirit of Simone, companions who are totally connected to their wild-child within. I want friends who are eager to play hooky, girlfriends who will linger at a coffee shop after dropping their kids at school, friends who know that thirty minutes of morning chitchat can make our day. We all need people in our lives who remind us to stop and notice the nuances of the present, comrades that prevent us from absently spinning from place to place. We all need people who make us laugh hard, people who don't fret if we chew and talk at the same time.

This year, four friends and I started the Ladies Who Lunch Club. We are five women who have professions and fourteen children among us, so we aren't really ladies who lunch, but now we are, once a month. On that designated day, a lunch we start looking forward to when we're paying the check from the last one, we dress up and let someone else cook and serve our food for a change. During these hour-and-a-half gab sessions, we applaud each other's work, kids, new haircuts, dreams. Oh, yeah, and we eat like we've been on a week-long fast. At Jaleo tapas bar in Washington, as we level a bowl of garlic mashed potatoes with four spoons, I am grateful for these middle-aged women who have not lost their knack for girl talk and giggling. We are the loudest table in an already very loud restaurant and are not self-consciously hushing each other. Let others be lifted by our laughter. Don't you ever become too busy to forget to laugh uproariously once in a while.

Remembering who you are can come in other simple and unexpected ways—taking an hour at dawn to walk on a path through the woods, savoring the sweet morning air. Remembering who you are can come from signing up your kids for ice skating lessons so you can skate with them, as you used to as a kid many a winter's afternoon. Remembering who I am meant going back to summer camp with our four sons, at the age of forty-five, as a group leader of forty seven- to nine-year-olds at Raquette Lake Boys Camp in the Adirondacks.

My editor Peggy Hackman in the Style section of *The Washington Post* asked me to write a piece on what going to camp felt like at middle age, an experience I repeated the next summer, and this excerpt is from that article, called "Postcard from Camp," written as if I were a child again, which is exactly how I felt. There is an intensity about camp, about breaking through physical and emotional limits in the wilderness, that makes me feel wilder than most anything else I've ever done.

Dear Mom:

We got back from summer camp late last night, and I'm sorry I didn't write sooner. But I was soooo busy canoeing and climbing the ropes course and chasing campers and playing with my friends, I didn't have time to breathe.

Mom, it was really fun.

I'm soooo sad to be home, sad as I used to be when I came home to Chicago each August after eight weeks at Camp Agawak. I loved camp then, soooo much, loved every day of my ten summers there. And I love camp now. Oh yeah, our children, your four grandsons, loved it, too.

I know you thought that going to summer camp at age forty-five was ridiculous; in fact, you laughed pretty hard when I told you that I'd been hired to work at Raquette Lake Boys Camp in Upstate New York. But when we invited that nice man to our house to show pictures and tell our boys about the camp, started in 1916 in the Adirondack mountains surrounded by a hilly forest of birch and pines, where kids do all kinds of sports and sing around campfires and come back year after year—well, I started having an out-of-body experience.

I was transported to the 1960s, to Agawak, to the birch and pine woods of Wisconsin, the place I was the happiest, lived the fullest, laughed the hardest, and made friends who I have to this day. I had a camp self and a city self, and the camp self is the person who felt, and feels, most like who I was meant to be.

I still tremble when I think about being Blue Team captain at Agawak, shooting bull's-eyes in archery, getting up on a slalom water ski for the first time, winning the horse show, stealing the flag from the White Team in Capture the Flag, socials with the boys camp across the lake. Lots of who I am today, the good parts and the mischievous parts, is because of stuff I did at camp. Nearly every night of their lives, our sons have been put to bed with soft anthems from Agawak sung by their mother, who has never really grown up, a mother who still plays jacks.

Ten summers of camp had given me two crucial life skills: tolerance and tenacity. When I was offered the job, I just started to cry. It was this karmic moment of total rightness where my life was coming full circle; the best of childhood was suddenly dangled in front of me. With gray hair and four children, I had a chance to live out an adult fantasy, to return to summer camp.

What else can I tell you? That the White Team won Color War. That s'mores taste as wonderful as they did twenty-five years ago. That swatting mosquitoes never felt so good. That I can't wait to go back.

Right now I'm unpacking our duffels filled with T-shirts and blue jeans that smell like dirt, pine, and fire. And I'm sitting here for the longest time with my face buried in the clothes, thinking about the several weeks I just spent being filthy and happy and wide-eyed. I'm thinking about Reveille playing at 7:30 A.M. and leaping out of bed, so excited to start a new day of waterfront and field sports that I wouldn't even change clothes, didn't need to really. With some nights and mornings below 50 degrees, I slept in sweats and wool socks and wore them the next day.

Don't worry—I did brush my teeth, and wore clean underwear, just like I told my campers to do. But I'm sure I looked yucky most of the summer, no makeup, snarly hair, that's the best part about camp really. You can be primal and beastly and nobody cares because most of them look worse than you do.

Mom, I'm forty-five but I feel fifteen, and I'm

getting really sad, thinking how the madness of autumn is about to steam-roll me out of this serene summer trance. After Labor Day, things just get nuts, for all of us. We get swallowed by our overscheduled lives instead of swimming in the moment, like you get to do at camp.

I gotta admit, after all this fun in a place where cell phones don't work and I was disconnected from email, I got behind in some of my work. But let me tell you—I got ahead in my life.

Love,
Iris

Many people I told about summer camp curled their lips as they remembered their own camp experiences of picking out ticks and shivering in tents during thunderstorms and swimming mandatory laps in Arctic-cold lakes. I tell those people that remembering who they are can be a lot more luxurious than the path I chose. Whatever you do, the goal is not to abandon your primal passions, to remember your dreams, to do your soul's work; it's the fire of life.

Reconnecting with the soul-seeds of self can be as simple as drawing a bath, pouring in some Dead Sea mineral salts, locking the door, lighting a patchouli candle, and sinking into nothingness, this while trying to transcend the cacophony of kids on the other side of the wall. It's a challenge I know only too well. After taking a delicious shower on a Sunday afternoon, my sons were clawing at the bathroom door, and their cries got me into such a tizzy that I gulped from what I thought was a bottle of mouthwash, swished the liquid around my mouth, then spit out, not Listerine, but Johnson's Baby Oil!

If we allow ourselves to be perpetually pulled by everyone else, without time for solitude and reflection, we are in danger of becoming Cordelia Grinstead, the forty-year-old heroine of Anne Tyler's novel *Ladder of Years*. Wife of a Baltimore doctor, mother of three, she feels suffocated by the demands of her life. So while the family is on vacation, she suddenly ditches them on the beach, and wearing only a bathing suit and beach robe, hitchhikes her way to a small town and creates a new self, far from the needy family she cannot endure for even one more second.

We all have urges to run away. But instead of abandoning your life, run away for a few hours and do something creative you used to do that made you feel good about yourself, like stringing African beads on a leather cord or dancing alone on the living room floor to the songs of the Supremes. I know too many men and women of middle age who don't dance anymore, who are in jobs or relationships they can't stand. They are sleeping too much, drinking too much, complaining they have no energy, no luster, no joy. Remember who you are.

Memories of all renditions of me envelop me at strange and random moments. Sometimes I am brushing my hair and I am remembering how good it felt when my mother brushed my hair with a clear blue plastic brush and braided it in two pigtails right above my ears. She pulled hard and it hurt when she sliced a perfect part in the back of my head with a sharp black comb. But I loved my braids, because getting my thick, curly hair styled into braids meant summer, and summer meant fun.

It is a 90-degree day in Tucson, Arizona, in April 2002, and I am brushing my hair and fastening it into a ponytail with the same kind of coated rubber bands my mother used. I feel a great surge of emotion, a blend of past and present and everything that is good and real.

It's hot like summer and my hair is back and my husband and four children are with me in the desert that I started exploring as soon as I could walk. The feeling of fullness is astounding, a mother and wife on spring break in Tucson reflecting on vacations as a child with her mother and father and a brother and a sister at the Double U Ranch, a rustic dude ranch that was transformed into the Canyon Ranch health spa in the early 1980s. At the Double U in the fifties and sixties and seventies, we would ride horses and square-dance and eat sweet oranges on our beds before our parents woke up. On my horse Chico, I would often ride the trail behind my father, who rode Ace, a black horse with one white eye. One year we came back to the ranch and Ace had died. My father died in 1986.

Standing in the desert today, my father and our old horses are alive as I show my young family the cactus and the Catalina Mountains, where I grew to love dry heat and the Southwest. I grab a fistful of tawny sand from near a saguaro and hunt for the tiny, rough garnets I used to find as a child. My sister Frances and I would let the sand stream through our fingers until only the tiny stones remained. They were the clear red of cranberries, a shade that remains my favorite color to this day. I wear a chunky silver ring inlaid with nine garnets, a ring I often hold up to the sunlight, and my whole girlhood streams through.

Wearing something, or surrounding yourself with things that evoke the best of your childhood is a direct link to the passion of your soul. What is hanging in your bedroom or living room that can bring you back to that sacred place? I have kept old paintings of kids on horses that hung in my childhood bedroom and scenes of cypress trees overhanging cliffs along the ocean from Big Sur, where I spent some wonder-weekends during college. Along with the garnet ring, I wear silver bracelets, lots of them, from a collection I started in Arizona during the early 1960s, of old turquoise pieces that have cracked with time. These objects make me feel like I'm home, really home, not just living in a house, but residing squarely in myself.

My college students laugh when I tell them to plug into their passion, and drink deeply of Washington, D.C., during their studies in the capital. They snicker that plugging into their passion sounds sexual, and that drinking deeply could mean hitting the bars of Georgetown. But they soon learn that what I really mean is to pay attention to every professor, to every subject, to every day and to what turns them on. And when a buzzer reverberates deep within, they need to heed that beckoning, because it's their heart and soul talking. The younger you are when you take action on your gut passion, the better off you are later in life. Too many people are floundering at fifty.

Self Beyond Career

Every move I've made in my education and career, I have stepped off something certain onto something secure, from Horace Mann School to Oak Park River Forest High School to an undergraduate degree from Stanford University in 1976. I then worked for several years at Margie Korshak public relations in Chicago before landing my first full-time journalism job, at the now-defunct *Dallas Times-Herald*. From Texas I moved to Washington, D.C., and a post as the national feature writer for United Press International. After getting married in 1988, I left UPI to become a freelance writer and stay home with four children, the first born in 1989, the second in 1991, and the twins arriving in 1993. When our children were all old enough to be in school, I became an assistant professor of journalism at American University, this while getting my master's degree in liberal studies at Georgetown University.

Spring semester 2002, I took time off from American University to research and compose *Surrendering to Yourself*. And in the process of writing about living your dreams and finding yourself beyond kids and career, I felt my own dreams rising. Every time I thought of returning to three days a week of teaching I felt a jab inside so penetrating that it would take my breath away. That sharp jab I have felt at different turns since I was a child has always meant stop, rethink, you can't do that! That gut jab is the siren song of truth.

Being away from the classroom has given me more time to write, and aside from my family, layering language into articles and books is what I love most in the world. As anyone who works from home will attest, it is glorious to shuffle from the breakfast table to your office, in a tattered bathrobe and flip-flops. I have also learned something that more experienced parents told me while I was writing *Surrendering to Motherhood* and three of the four kids were in diapers. I heard over and over that if I thought it was hard raising infants and toddlers, just wait until the children started hitting their teens. My oldest son is about to turn thirteen, and I can tell you it's never been more crucial to be home as much as I can, to watch, to listen, to run interference. Too many teens are obsessed with looking cool to their peers, and I know it's my premier job right now to make sure my adolescent son worries first about being cool to himself, aiming for self-love and self-acceptance over approval.

I made a hard phone call to my longtime boss, Dean David Brown, and set up a meeting. Seated on the striped couch in his office, I told this man that I loved my job, but couldn't return quite yet to my professor position in the program called Washington Journalism Semester, because I needed to write more myself. In three days of giving my students new journalism skills, I was often ignoring my own journalistic growth.

I shared with him a plan that had been percolating for a while, a way to stay connected to American University and Washington, D.C., a thrilling artery of life. My idea was to do a two-hour writing seminar once a week. That way I could keep my hand in teaching college students, which has always been invigorating and is a way of giving back, and still have enough time to write myself. During the course of an animated conversation, we created a new part-time position for me. I was jubilant. It was the perfect solution. You can get what you want if you know what you want, and what you don't want.

On the hour-long ride from Washington back to our home near the Chesapeake Bay, I listened to Aretha Franklin singing about some man making her feel like a natural woman. I have always loved that song, but that afternoon it struck me: Why should it take the attention of a man to feel like a natural woman? We should feel natural and powerful on our own, which I was experiencing in a blast at that moment following my conversation with Dave Brown. For the first time since donning cap and gown in 1976, on a sultry June day in Palo Alto, California, I was stepping not onto something else, not onto an external rung on the ascent to success, but onto myself, onto a notch deeply embedded within.

I am reminded of Mrs. Annie Johnson, a character from

Maya Angelou's *Wouldn't Take Nothing for My Journey Now* who lives in Arkansas in the early 1900s. Unhappily married, she and her husband split up—he claims God was calling him to Enid, Oklahoma, to become a preacher, but doesn't tell her the preacher he was going to study with had an unmarried daughter who had turned his head. Annie keeps their one-room house, and her husband walks out with most of the cash.

Angelou tells the tale:

> *Annie, over six feet tall, big-boned, decided that she would not go to work as a domestic and leave her "precious babes" to anyone else's care. There was no possibility of being hired at the town's cotton gin or lumber mill, but maybe there was a way to make the two factories work for her. In her words, "I looked up the road I was going and back the way I come, and since I wasn't satisfied, I decided to step off the road and cut me a new path."*
>
> *Each of us has the right and responsibility to assess the roads which lie ahead, and those over which we have traveled. And if the future road looms ominously or unpromising, and the roads back uninviting, then we need to gather our resolve and, carrying only the necessary baggage, step off that road into another direction.*

Stepping off the road, and cutting herself a new path, Annie opens up a stand selling homemade ham and chicken pies to the town's factory workers on an empty lot behind the cotton gin. Fried in boiling fat and wrapped in newspaper, her pungent pies sell for a nickel apiece, and they are so popular she enlarges her shop and increases her inventory to include cheese, cookies, candy, fruit, coal, oil, and even leather soles for shoes.

Although cutting a new path can initially mean having more faith than money, by trusting our gut instincts we can never be led astray. What is your gut telling you right now? Is your job a good fit? Does it make you feel like a natural woman or man? If your gut is knotted, burning, thrashing, something is terribly wrong. No one should suffocate their self of truth in a misfit job or relationship. You get only one life to get it right.

Turning Within for Power and Strength

When I was in seventh grade and passionate about everything, Miss Verna Happel gave us the assignment to put together a lengthy booklet on the career we would like to pursue. I wanted to be a journalist and a doctor and own a horse ranch in Arizona but decided to write about becoming a volunteer in the Peace Corps, because in that job you get to do lots of different things—teach people, visit foreign lands, mingle with various cultures and personalities. I did not join the Peace Corps, but journalism certainly combines those qualities as well, and as I read through this booklet today, written thirty-six years ago, I am struck by how I did stay true to, and focused on, what turned me on as a preteen.

Focus and passion are a powerful combination leading toward becoming engaged and productive, not only in work, but in all of life. Focus and passion takes you from the realm of the ordinary into the extraordinary. What's more frightening: the uncertainty of exploring uncharted territory, or the certainty that if you stay put, you're imprisoned in mediocrity? And the longer you're behind those bars, the harder it is to break out.

In Beryl Markham's biography *West with the Night*, this author, who was one of the first women to receive a commercial pilot's license—and in 1936 became the first person to fly across the Atlantic from east to west—writes something every child should have tacked up on his or her bulletin board: "I learned what every dreaming child needs to know—that no horizon is so far that you cannot get above it or beyond it."

I was talking to an investment broker, age forty-four, who wants to become an interior designer. She is paralyzed in indecision at the prospect of walking away from a six-figure salary: "The older I get, the harder it is to take risks," she said. Everyone who knows this woman and has been entertained in her Baltimore home is impressed by her taste in furniture and room decor and her knack for setting a spectacular table. She is style personified.

I told her that if she walked potential clients through her own house they would hire her on the spot, that she obviously loves to make things beautiful, and with passion would come the power to create a successful design firm. At this writing, she is still sitting on the fence, but she is leaning toward her own backyard, and trying to start her own business.

How can we know if a new venture will pan out unless we give it a try? This interior designer stuck in the wrong job is eager to set herself free, but her body won't yet yield to the whispers of her soul. She can always go back to investing if things don't pan out—if not at the same firm, then somewhere else. But she can never go back to this moment, this midlife urge to test new waters, to let dreams fly. A great time to test dreams is at forty-four, when you still have half your life left to turn around.

Who would you want to be if you weren't who you are? If you don't stop to answer that question in your forties or fifties, there's always your sixties.

Barbara Lamborn's girlhood dream of becoming a model was abruptly yanked out from under her when she was nineteen. She traveled from rural Maryland to the Eileen Ford Agency in New York City and was told, "No, you won't do in this business." But Lamborn, now seventy-three, five-foot-ten with ash blond hair and striking in a clingy white T-shirt, never abandoned her dreams of strutting down a runway, which she recently did in bridal shows for Nordstrom. She is now registered with several modeling agencies along the East Coast and has appeared in numerous print ads and television commercials, including one touting a casino in which she can be seen jitterbugging.

A grandmother of twelve, Lamborn has also had bit

parts in two movies, a Korean film and *Minority Report*, directed by Steven Spielberg and starring Tom Cruise. She weight-trains, is an avid cyclist, and is more fit than she's ever been, claiming that seventy-three "doesn't feel that different than any other age." I spoke to her as she was about to leave on a fifty-mile bike trip near Salisbury, Maryland, with her eighty-four-year-old husband, Bob. Ten years ago they rode their bikes across the country, from Los Angeles to Boston.

I don't feel old. In many ways, I've never been in better shape. Certainly my work is exciting, it's a dream really, to be doing modeling now, after all these years. And to be this strong physically, this is new for me, too. As a child I had severe asthma, I couldn't do any running around. So it's unusual for me to be strong and fit. I've never been athletic, and I have discovered that I like being an athlete very much. So yes, I am taking care of myself in ways I never did before. I was always drawn to fashion and intrigued with the idea of modeling. I don't know why; here I was just a skinny, very unglamorous kid, but there was glamour in my heart.

While I was in college I did some modeling for my parents' corset and bra shop in downtown Baltimore and the ads appeared in the Baltimore Sun. *I remember that first trip to New York with my mother to see Eileen Ford. We took the train. And I was crushed when they rejected me. I went in a different direction but remained in the fashion field. I taught classes at the Barbizon School and dancing at Arthur Murray, and starting a successful image consulting business that taught corporate men and women how to project a profes-*

sional image. We gave Assertive Appearance seminars across the country.

The idea to try modeling again came to me years later as I was leafing through the yellow pages and saw an advertisement for a business that helped people enter the modeling field. I made an appointment and was told to get some photographs done, and they suggested agencies to take them to in Washington, Baltimore, and Virginia. I was signed right away. My first job was for a retirement village in Pennsylvania, and I turned out to be on the cover of their brochure, sitting at an easel, in a straw hat, with a paintbrush in my hand.

Once I began, it was all very exciting. Of course I'm well aware that I'm a model of over seventy and not a model of twenty. The older I get, the more I realize everything is just going at once. The face, the body, you can't keep up with trying to look younger and younger, and I'm certainly not interested in plastic surgery. Why get your face lifted when everything else on your body is not lifted? Your hands will always look your age.

I once spoke to this ninety-year-old woman who had played the piano for years for a ballet company, and she just fascinated me, because when she retired at the age of sixty-five she decided it was time to go really live her life. So she learned how to play the mandolin and got herself sexy little outfits and taught herself how to lift her face through exercise. And I learned that from her, and it has helped me look the best that I can look at seventy-three. But at my age, you cannot have your self-esteem rely on how you look. It's all about how you feel inside. So I believe the best thing I can do is to be as strong *physically as I can be, and to find contentment on a more pro-found level. It wouldn't be me to be a grandmother who stays home, baking cookies. This person I am right now feels very true to who I am. I've had this interest since I was sixteen.*

I am grateful that I was undeterred when I was turned away from the Ford Agency. Because fifty years later, here I am. I am thrilled to be pushing my potential to see what I can do at this stage of my life. I have also recently joined an anti-aging medical program, and I am taking vitamins, minerals, and natural hormones. It greatly intrigues me that I have the power to do things right now to restore my body, not to the way it was—I'm not unrealistic—but to be the very best that I can be. Really, I'm in better shape now than ever, in all areas.

This morning I was on the treadmill for thirty minutes, and as I was struggling away I remembered how my asthma kept me from doing any running. I've never done any sus-tained aerobics like this in my life. And I am very interested now in pursuing bodybuilding. The modeling just adds another dimension.

Going about my everyday life, I don't feel glamorous. It's not like heads are turning. But when you go on a modeling job, no matter what corporation it's for, when you walk in the front door and say to the receptionist, "I'm here for the photo shoot; I am the model," mouths do drop open and you are treated in almost a royal way. It feels nice.

I cannot say that I have reinvented myself at this age, but there has definitely been a refinement of self. That's one of the main things that attracted me to modeling. It is a force to help me to be constantly the best that I can be. It's a force to eat right,

*stand up straight, and be in good shape and to explore avenues
that I might not otherwise explore. So in a way it's an enforced
discipline.*

*I look back at what my parents did for me, and I think
they supported me in whatever I wanted to do, even though as
a teenager, my mother thought modeling was one of my foolish dreams that would pass. But she used to always say about
me when I was young, "Oh, we don't have to worry about Barbara. She's just going to dance through life."*

*And I do feel that way now. There are many new things in
my life in older age. But as far as living to a hundred, whether
I do or not, my real wish and hope is that if I do, I'm healthy
until I die. And I think there are things that we can all do to
preserve ourselves and I'm just eager to do everything I can.
I'm on the right path and I'm going against a lot of people's
beliefs as far as taking all the vitamins and minerals and hormones, but I'm doing what I feel intuitively is right.*

*I would tell other people in their seventies who want to
begin anew that it takes a lot of courage to go against the status quo. It takes a lot of courage to do things that your friends
aren't doing and probably never will do. You just have to take
a deep breath and do what you think is right for you.*

Taking a deep breath and doing what you think is right
doesn't have to be as major as taking on a new career as a
septuagenarian. It can be superficial pampering. I just
painted my fingernails with coral pink polish, a gaudy shade
by Opi called Arrivederci. This week in February in Maryland has hovered in the seventies, so I felt like shedding the

Cabernet red nails of winter, and being daring. I can't stop looking at my fingertips that appear to be dipped in a mixture of orange and raspberry sherbets, trying to decide if I love this new shade or hate it.

Sitting at the kitchen table, I splay my hands, turn them over, and look again with bent fingers, then hold them up to the sunlight. The color is Caribbean hot, yet I'm a red person, not a pink person, and the effect feels weird. Just when I'm thinking I hate Arrivederci, ten-year-old Isaac comes in, stands at my shoulder, looks at my hands, then smiles.

"It's *you*, Mommy. It's tropical," he says.

I ask him what it means to be tropical.

"Warm and fun."

Of course I instantly start to love my fingernails because I think of warmth and fun and coral pink shells. So I must have chosen this shade from the dozens of bottles on the shelf straight from the gut, that touchstone within that dictates truth of self, the instinct that told Barbara Lamborn to keep trying to be a model. Long after Isaac has gone, I stay at the kitchen table, staring at my nails, thinking about what else I am, what people think I am, and how closely those two streams intersect. My husband, Chuck, says the choice of nail polish should not be interpreted as something profound, but women know there are colors that feel right and colors that feel wrong. When a friend says "This looks like you" while we're shopping and the clothing item is a dress I would never wear, I realize that this friend doesn't know me so well after all. I know me well, and more and more, that's who I ask for advice.

Many people lumber through the days and years and decades without honestly appraising who they are and what they genuinely want out of life. They get lost in other people, consumed by material riches, or fooled by their own plastic surgery. But we cannot run from our true selves forever. Inevitably, something jolts us into our naked being. And in that naked being is where we need to go, it's our true home.

"Normally we seek happiness outside ourself," writes Geshe Kelsang Gyatso in *Introduction to Buddhism.* "We try to obtain better material conditions, a better job, higher social status. . . . In his Dharma teachings, Buddha advises us not to seek happiness outside ourselves but to establish it within our mind. . . . Then, no matter how difficult our external circumstances may be, we shall always be happy and peaceful."

Even the luckiest of us, those who have managed thus far to escape difficult external circumstances, will eventually be catapulted into a moment when it feels like our world suddenly collapses. This flight into self must come before your last child goes off to college and you are suddenly faced with an empty house with lots of mirrors and unfinished business you can no longer avoid.

My nest is still crowded with young boys and noise, but I think about an empty nest every day. In the mornings, before the children go off to school, all four of them ride around the driveway on their bicycles, a fast-moving circle, around and around, and I stare at them through the kitchen window, a giant mug of coffee in my hand. Lately, with five-foot-eight Theo leading the pack, I can't look at our sons, laughing and hollering, or at their backpacks in a sloppy pile near the car, without choking up with tears. I yearn to freeze time, this early twilight of motherhood, when I still have control over what they eat, what they wear, where they go, who they invite over for play dates. I am terrified of the day when they will no longer permit their mother to bury her face in their hair and fuss over them and squeeze them, as if they were rag dolls.

I am determined, in this shaky moment when I can't look at my growing children without crying, to break through this awful feeling that when they leave, my own self will leave. I am working hard on my own growth into a woman who loves her family fiercely but does not need them to survive. When my father died, I was thirty-one, and for the first two years I did not go one day without dissolving into sobs. I could not look at an empty chair without imagining that he was sitting in it. I'd see a tall, older man on the street with a high forehead like his, wearing his type of trench coat, and thought I would die. There were many times when I did think that dying would be the only way I could ever get over the agony of losing this man who was the smart and adoring pillar of my existence.

The pain and despondency numbed with time, and I married a smart and adoring man who gave me four children, sons who will never know their grandfather and who have the same hold over my heart that he had. Yet I never again want to feel that I will die if someone I love dies. And so I am learning to brace myself in my own self, knowing that black days are ahead, days of loss, and that I will carry on. My father is gone and my boys on bicycles are here—for how long, I do not know. What I *do* know is that I have this day and my soul and my dreams of books to be written, and that needs to be enough.

"There is within each of us a modulation, an inner exaltation, which lifts us above the buffetings with which events assail us," wrote Albert Schweitzer in an essay called *Reverence*. "Hence, our dependence upon events is not absolute; it is qualified by our spiritual freedom. Therefore, when we speak of resignation it is not sadness to which we refer, but the triumph of our will to live over whatever happens to us. And to become ourselves, to be spiritually alive, we must have passed beyond this point of resignation."

Here's one simple method for triumphing in your own will to live in the face of adversity, advice that came from my dad and ironically helped me heal after his death. When I was feeling sad about anything—a C on a test, a friend who had slighted me, a bad boyfriend, general blahs, Theodore Krasnow would tell me to go into my bathroom, close the door, look in the mirror, and shout "I'm great, I'm great, I'm great!" He said not to come out until I had said it thirty times. And so I would do it. Sometimes I'd be crying at first, but as it always turned out, when I had made it to thirty, I'd be laughing, a full-throttle laugh that would pump me with life and power. I always walked out of that bathroom believing I was great, and ready again to take on life.

Our power and strength are not exterior to our being; they are right inside of us. We can claim power by believing "I'm great, I'm great." This fragment from a poem by Derek Walcott speaks to the power of loving what you see in the mirror:

Sit. Feast on your life.

I'm thinking about feasting on life as I walk through the woods near our house, savoring the dawn and the black-eyed Susans and the most wonderful damp forest smell, fresh from a rain. It's only me and the rising sun until I see a small, bearded man crouched low, foraging under a moss-laden log. He looks like a troll. I walk up to him and watch quietly as he knits his fingers through the ground. Curious, entranced, I ask him what he is doing.

"I'm looking for mushrooms," he tells me in a whisper. He unzips a small canvas pouch and shows off a dozen morels as if they are rubies; he has gathered these over the course of a five-mile, two-hour walk that started before five A.M. I continue to listen as he explains how to spot a patch of woods where these delicate mushrooms may sprout, and how he feels the thrill of a treasure hunter when he's look-ing for them. As someone who thought that exquisite morels grew only in the south of France, I feel like finding him is a treasure. He keeps talking and I'm enchanted as he shares a recipe for mushrooms and chicken and red wine.

So I learned on this morning, when I was drinking deeply of the moment and taking the time for some self-affirming solitude, that we live along a trail where gourmet mushrooms can be found. And I met a man who takes the time to indulge in a simple passion of his soul—which he says balances his life as a car salesman. Do mushrooms grow near you?

Self Beyond Motherhood

There are many mothers who spend all their time forming the identities of their children and ignoring their own growth. Their kids become who they are: "My children are my essence," one woman told me, and I have felt this time and time again myself, a blurring of my own self with the selves of my sons. I have been that woman who when asked "How are you?" promptly reports how the children are, what they're doing, how big they have gotten, their update in sports.

Although the love for my children is all-encompassing and all-consuming, I have always kept writing, the work of my soul. The happiest mothers I interviewed for *Surrendering to Motherhood* who had abandoned offices were those who kept a hand dipped in their professions, such as a pastry chef who left her catering firm but started a home-based bakery.

I'm thrilled that I still have my journalism, as I'm raising sons who now call me Mom more than Mommy. My twelve-year-old wipes my kisses off his cheek; this is the child who spent the first three years of his life sleeping between Chuck and me. He is separating, sometimes defiantly. He shuts his bedroom door behind him and retreats to check his emails or play electric guitar. Soon I will be writing letters to children enrolled in colleges far away, sons who may have body pierces and girlfriends and no homesickness at all. And so on this day, even if it's more than a decade before all of our children graduate high school, I must bolster myself beyond motherhood, for what's to come. The real empty nest—confronting clean bedrooms with comforters pulled tightly and Hot Wheels in boxes, not strewn on the rugs—will leave less of a lonely sting if we have exciting selves for company.

This is not me-ism in the selfish sense, it's me-ism in a survival sense. We will crumble if we don't have a fortified self to fall back on when the people we depend on for worth and love leave home. An empty life in an empty house is a surefire path to a total breakdown. We can't lose ourselves when the Mommy self dies. When the babies started coming for me, four in three years, my pre-motherhood self became a distant and diffused memory. I remember one December afternoon while I was nursing newborn twins, a one-year-old and three-year-old yanking at me, feeling euphoric and miserable. Part of it was hormonal letdown, but most of all it was a meltdown of self. Who was I? Part robot, part cow, totally discombobulated. Years later, I still have miles to go before Mommy isn't the dominant role in my psyche, I found out recently.

Last spring I took a two-day trip alone to the nearby Delaware shore—no kids, no husband, no computer. The goal was to separate myself from my family and do some probing and reflecting, apart from my role as wife and mother. I chose as my destination the beach house in Bethany that our family has rented every summer since Theo was a baby, and when I opened the door, twelve years of sandy children came at me, in an avalanche of emotion and clarity. Although they were two hours away with their dad, they still filled the house that contains all our summers.

I saw Jack and Zane walking for the first time, Isaac and Theo flinging water balloons at each other on the porch, brown faces with cookie-dough ice cream dripping down their chins. I saw diapers and baseballs and surfboards. I saw my whole fourteen-year married life displayed before me, like a meteorite shower, the past beamed everywhere. I wasn't alone, I was six people, as I always am in Bethany.

As I sat on the screen porch overlooking the Atlantic Ocean, I thought how huge is the role of my family in shaping my identity, and how that is good and that is bad. When you still have children at home, you are so immersed in where you are, you don't stop and think about who you will be when they go. But they leave and then you are stuck, bare, and alone. I'm not yet ready to know naked aloneness. But I know it awaits me, and I am increasingly less afraid of it.

I go down to the beach the next morning and it's windy and cool, and I put my red-striped beach chair at the lip of the ocean. The sand blows in my face and the cold is a slap into this moment where I am a woman of middle age sitting by herself. I could be anyone, a widow, the childless president of a steel company. Gulls fly overhead and a white cigarette boat blasts by. I am hypnotized by the sky that is endless and blue, dusted with chalky clouds, transparent and arched upward, like a smile. For about twelve minutes I am serene, lulled by the waves and the silence and the salty air. And then a mother walks by trailed by a small child, who is wearing an animal-print FlapHappy hat with safari flaps like the kind all our boys wore; and I'm missing my kids intensely. Who am I beyond my children? I do not know, but I need to know. How can I know? They are me, I'm thinking, seated on a chair in a spot where I've watched them August after August dance in and out of the sea like puppies, shrieking.

I stand and I stretch and I cry. Beyond missing them, I am grieving for the progressive loss of a Mommy self, who is now Mom. I'm grieving for the red-cushioned rocking chair that no one sits in anymore and where I nursed four babies. I'm wary of the formidable task that looms: Without four small children pulling at me and needing me, who am I meant to be now?

I fold up the beach chair and walk slowly to the house, savoring the soft sand and the cold wind and the pinecone-laden path to the house. I fling open the door and hear the familiar squeak, and again I am flooded with a dozen summers: this porch, these pines, this ocean where I can never be alone. My chest feels tight and I can't sit still. Should I pack up, get in the car, and go back home? I call Chuck and tell him that Bethany Beach is not somewhere I can be without our family. And he tells me: "Stay there. It's beautiful. Do what you went there to do."

Do what you went there to do—sounds like an order

from Carlos Castaneda. Well, I came here to get to know the person who I'm going to live with forever, a self I've been trying to run away from, I see this now. I sit frozen by the phone at the counter in the kitchen where the boys eat their chocolate doughnuts from the bakery down the road. I am remembering me at twenty-one and twenty-six and thirty, moving from Chicago to Dallas to Washington, D.C., racing between interviews, hailing cabs and shouting addresses, slamming out stories on deadline. This afternoon, looking out on an empty beach and not expected to be anywhere, I sigh from a weariness that is bone deep. It's an immobilizing exhaustion, that throbs and hurts, yet with my breaths comes relief: I've stopped running; there is nowhere higher to go; this is it, at the counter, on the beach, all alone. I feel a gratitude I haven't felt before, because it's only in stillness that you can give thanks to the spiritual powers that bring you to the place where you are, and I've never been this still before.

As if in a trance, I lumber from the kitchen to the nearest bed, which is the bottom bunk in a room where the walls are rough wood and the kids get splinters. Sun streams across my black bathing suit as I stretch out on the blue cotton blanket and sink into the deepest of sleeps, a sleep that comes not only from the day's heavy thinking but from a lifetime of moving too fast.

Five hours later, I'm a new person at the Parkway restaurant eating a Caesar salad and drinking red wine with Lara Bellistri, a young woman who used to baby-sit our sons and now has her own toddler, Hannah. And I'm thinking of Chuck telling me: Do what you went there to do. Having supper with an old friend, flushed with sunburn and wine, I am okay in Bethany Beach, Delaware, my summer home. Lara's tiny daughter is on her lap, grabbing at french fries, and I'm thinking not of our sons as babies, but of my next stage, the renaissance and reinvention that comes with middle age. I am excited for who I am to happen again in a new way, for the inevitable shedding of selves that happens for women, cyclical animals who are destined to keep changing.

I am woman, and thank God for that. Right now I'm having fun, after a day of cerebral torture. When I talk to Chuck later that night, he says, "You sound too good."

The next day on the beach, the sky and the sea are placating and uplifting, and not a backdrop for sharp memories that bring me down. As a father strolls by with his toddler in a backpack carrier, I think about Lara's child and how a baby requires constant and unrelenting care. I am happy that our four babies are increasingly self-sufficient; the heaviness of young motherhood has lifted, and there are parts that are sad, but more parts that are sweet. I thank Chuck profusely for giving me this gift of forty-eight-hours alone, and also Helen Gutmann, the woman who owns the beach house and let me stay there during off-season as an early birthday present.

Do what you went there to do, I'm hearing Chuck say, and I'm doing it—bracing myself in myself. I came to know the loneliness of empty nest before I am faced with an empty nest. I came to think about what it would be like when my mother passes on and I am an orphan. I came to place an anchor within, so that when loved ones do move out or die, I will not die inside. In Bethany, alone, I surrender to this unrelenting truth, that life can be debilitating and that all I can do is love people in this moment, stay aligned to my soul, and do good work. I will not curl up and surrender when obstacles are hurled my way; rather, I surrender to my self, and she can get me through anything.

On this short beach trip away from my hub of civilization, I can't compare myself to an Arctic explorer living in an ice cave for months or to a climber in the Himalayas, out for a mountaintop epiphany. The weather in Delaware is warm, and I'm in a comfortable house and there is Brie and Coronas in my refrigerator. But I'm searching for something, just as these adventurers are, and I believe that as humans we all seek the same things: peace and purpose and challenge. And yes, at Bethany, I am experiencing an epiphany of sorts, one that is not coming at me in a startling flash, but slowly washing over me, with the rhythm of the waves. A man in a red kayak is skimming the water out in the distance, and I'm remembering the red kayaks from Camp Agawak and skimming across Blue Lake in Wisconsin. In my thoughts, I am an unencumbered child, not a mother of four trying to come out from under an avalanche of memories.

I go back into the house for lunch and the languor of the moment is shaken again by a flashback. The sun is streaming across a rough pine wall, and the red-brown wood turns scarlet. It's that wall aflame with red where we used to put the crib, and I see Jack at nine months, standing up in a purple T-shirt, with a pacifier in his mouth, a shard of sunlight spraying his cheek. And behind that hallucination is an empty corner where we used to hang Theo's Big Bird windsock, and I remember holding my firstborn so he could bat at the funny, yellow bird with his chubby fists. I wince at these mental snapshots of babies who are now boys who put on headphones and listen to Lenny Kravitz. I sit in a rocking chair on the porch, rocking myself back into this moment now. There is a lush growth of dune grass in front of me, and the willowy fronds are swaying. Their whisper in the wind is the only sound.

The last time I was alone on a beach for two days was in Big Sur, California, in 1976. I was twenty-one, nestled by cypress tree-covered cliffs, in a halter top and torn blue-jean skirt. I was searching then and searching right now, in a way I haven't been able to do for years, particularly not in Bethany, where the yelps of children drown out any voice from within, and where there is usually no urge to ponder the nature of existence because existence takes care of itself. We eat, swim, laugh, eat, sleep. And I clean up messes, wet clothes, sticky counters, sand-encrusted showers. My only chore today is to excavate a self that has been consumed by relationships.

It is impossible to hear the soul if you don't stop, even for a day or two, and disconnect from the world. I mean really disconnect, from email and faxes and beepers, and connect with what's crying out inside of you. I am clear of my own cry right now, and it is to discover a self beyond the labels *mom, wife, writer*. Whatever titles you hold, parent, attorney, teacher, nurse—make sure you too are trying to know the self beyond your job description.

Your children are not you. Your spouse is not you. Your job is not you. And until you consciously go there, dig there, move the other stuff out of the way for a while, and hang out with yourself, the you of truth remains a buried jewel. A week later I am back home, husband and sons are asleep and I am watching my Folger's Colombian coffee dripping into the plastic pot. I pour myself a mug, stir in heavy cream and a heaping teaspoon of honey. The syrupy brew, which is just the way I like it, jolts me into wakefulness as I take in the full moon, and the charcoal sky. The moon turns into a sun that seeps into my skin, and I'm thinking how morning is virginal and beckoning, how everything seems possible.

I go back to some of my Bethany Beach resolutions and recommit to becoming a person who slows down and sits and really listens to her heart. Aloneness, at 6:10 A.M. on this day, feels glorious. I close my eyes and sink deeper into the island of self, when a little voice says, "Hi, Mom. It's Jack." Jack has been shaken by a bad dream, so I pick him up and stroke his body covered in gray fleece pajamas. He is holding my neck so tightly I can hardly breathe.

I carry Jack back upstairs and put him in bed next to Theo, and he curls up next to his big brother's back. And I stand at the door and watch my biggest and smallest sons, as Jack quickly falls asleep and Theo tosses a bit. I kiss each of them on the forehead and go fetch my coffee, which is now cold, and my head is again filled with children, my children, all children, the fragility of this life. We share a common, grieving heart with parents across the world who are burying children from wars and famine, and with parents in this country whose children are missing, taken from their beds while the family slept peacefully.

This could be any of us. We'll get our turns, it may not be as severe, but our own unblemished, insular spheres, to be sure, will be pocked with some tragedy. Do you have a deep reservoir of self to dive into for solace and strength? I'm digging furiously to get there. I saw Goldie Hawn on the *Tonight* show recently. She was telling Jay Leno about lying by her swimming pool in California and being overwhelmed by emptiness. Her children are grown, her partner Kurt Russell was not home, and as Hawn said, "It's only me. It's only me." Of course, we do not feel pity for Goldie Hawn being alone in a mansion with lots of money in the bank. But the words "It's only me" and the image of a mother alone in her house are striking.

The lesson from Hawn is that your children might depend on you for everything right now, but they aren't sticking by forever: eventually it's only you. "It's only me" can feel like a rich prospect or can fill you with dread. What will you do when the children leave home? It's the day before Mother's Day, and I'm swimming with the twins, one on my hip, one on my back. A woman sitting at the edge of the pool is petting the head of a little boy who appears to be of kindergarten age. She nuzzles his cheek and then pets him some more, and I'm saying to her in my mind, "Enjoy this second, because it's shorter than you can imagine."

Silky-cheeked children turn into teenagers with stubble. They leave and we stay; then what? Theo already puts gel in his hair and his voice is so husky I can't recognize it on the phone, this boy whose birth I remember as if it were ten minutes ago, coming quickly, open-eyed, nearly thirteen years ago.

Today, in the heat of summer, I watch him take command of the basketball court, passing the ball through his legs, then jumping to the rim and dunking it, twanging the basket with his fingers. He is more man than boy, and I'm reminded of horses I have ridden that push their head so far forward the reins in my hand are tight, they burn my skin, these horses who want control of their own heads, and their own pace.

Soon four sons will be tightening the reins, and the worn leather straps will break free from my grasp. Yesterday I asked Theo to join me on my walk through the woods, and I was surprised when he said yes, thinking we'd get forty-five minutes alone to talk. No sooner had we hit the trail than he shot out in a sprint in front of me, looking over his shoulder with a you'll-never-catch-me grin. I am walking as fast as I can, and he is running, swiftly and with grace, like a buck. As I watch, Theo's silhouette become smaller and smaller and I imagine looking out my car window as we drive away from a college campus in six short years, taking him to begin his freshman year. He'll again be leaving his mother behind in the dust.

My children are my essence; but they are not my whole, they are not my soul. Are you letting go? We need to before we're rattling around a vacant house.

CAN BOTOX FIX YOUR SOUL?

I'm lifting weights in a gym and the woman next to me tells me she just lost 25 pounds in two months because she wanted to be thin for her thirtieth high school reunion next month. As she puts it: "I was this weight when I graduated from high school, and I wanted to go back as the old me."

Pumping and panting, I think of this concept of the old me versus the new me. I love the muscles and energy that weight lifting gives me, it is absolutely a kick-in-the-butt and a kick for the spirit. But I harbor no delusions that when I'm thin, I am a totally different me than when I delivered twins and weighed 50 pounds more than this. We do not change our fundamental core by altering the packaging. If you don't love her at 175 pounds, you will not love her at 125. I quit weighing myself two years ago and it's been great. The numbers on the scale had the audacity to ruin my day; now I weigh in with myself, and if I feel healthy, then I'm doing fine.

I'm sitting on a dock in Cambridge, Maryland, feet dangling in the water, and I take out my small mirror to apply sunscreen to my face. The harsh glare of the midday sun reflecting off the Choptank River shows every line on my face. I am particularly captivated by the tiny lines above my upper lip. When did I get those? I feel so young; do I look old?

The first lip lines I noticed on a woman were on my octogenarian grandmother. Her bright red lipstick used to form rivulets in those lines above her lip. A fifty-year-old friend of mine tells me she started outlining the bow of her lips in pencil to confine the color when her first lines appeared. I tell another friend, age forty-nine, that I'm old enough now to need lip pencil, and she tells me to forget it and go straight for the Botox. She's been getting injections between her eyebrows and around her lips for two years. This is a very attractive woman with a body taut from kick-boxing. She is all but wrinkle-free, but her face looks strained. "It's hard to stop," she admits of the tune-ups necessary every few months when the effect of the treatment wears off.

As I write this, Botox is all over the news because botu-linum toxin type A, a sterile form of the poison that causes botulism and when injected eases wrinkles and tightens flaccid necks, has just been approved for cosmetic use by the Food and Drug Administration. The fact that Botox was still in the testing stage didn't stop the hundreds of thousands of people who have already received the treatment, and it's a green light for the throngs, who may have been wary, to line up at outpatient plastic surgery centers. Botox fans say they are happier, yet often it's hard to see real joy in their expressions because many of their laugh lines have disappeared. Director Martin Scorsese complained that he can't find actresses over fifty who have faces with moving parts to show emotion.

I don't love lip lines or the furrow between my brows; my eyes melt into a fan of wrinkles when I smile. But I choose not to try and eliminate my hard-earned etchings of time, because I would like to accept myself exactly as I am at each stage of aging, so there are no surprises later on. That's the reason I don't dye my gray hair. That a mature woman who ages naturally is no longer sexy is a male-perpetuated myth that we need to throw a united sister-hood behind to abolish. One of the sexiest, most genuine women on the screen is Meryl Streep, who is not skeletal, who has a prominent nose she has not tinkered with, and who is one hot babe at any age. A woman over fifty who is wise and passionate is more beautiful than a thirty-four-year-old with a tight face and an empty life. Botox tem-porarily erases wrinkles, it does not fix your soul.

Hanging in my office is a black-and-white postcard portrait of Georgia O'Keeffe. She is cloaked in black and her face is propped up in one hand, leathery and ancient, but there is a childlike curiosity in her eyes. This artist who painted poetry into sunsets and cattle skulls lived hard and sensuously until age ninety-eight, in the desolate paradise of Ghost Ranch in Abiquiu, New Mexico, and with the com-panionship of an assistant named Juan Hamilton, who was fifty-eight years younger. I interviewed Hamilton when he visited the National Gallery years ago to announce an

O'Keeffe retrospective, and here is how he described the spirited and "beautiful" woman he considered his best friend during her eighties and nineties.

"She went to bed early and she got up early and she ate well and she exercised," recalled Hamilton, her six-foot-two apprentice with thick chestnut hair. "That's how she lived to be ninety-eight. She enjoyed walking. She enjoyed a good fire. She enjoyed music. She did not have that self-destructive quality that many artists have.

"She was very strong and she lasted a long time," he added. "She did it so well, too. She never complained. She was so stoic until the very end. She never felt sorry for herself." It was Hamilton who encouraged O'Keeffe to paint into her nineties, despite her near blindness.

Georgia O'Keeffe's old face may not be a universal standard of female beauty. Yet her life beyond the flesh is a lesson for all of us on the importance of forging on and not feeling sorry for ourselves, focusing on living, not on looking perfect. From her first foray into the art world in the early 1900s, O'Keeffe had passion and purpose, and she attracted acolytes of all ages, who were transfixed by her energy and productivity. Growing up in Sun Prairie, Wisconsin, roused by the broad rolling hills and the great presence of nature, O'Keeffe—like Louise Nevelson—knew from early childhood that she wanted to be an artist. When she moved to Amarillo, Texas, to teach art at what is now West Texas State University, O'Keeffe wrote of the sun-drenched plains in a letter to a friend: "The plains, the wonderful great big sky, make me want to breathe so deep that I'll break . . ." The subdued and tasteful nudes of a young O'Keeffe shot by her husband Alfred Stieglitz are more erotic than any airbrushed, augmented Playmate of the Month.

O'Keeffe breathed so deep for so long, but didn't break ever, because she remained connected to her soul's longing for artistic expression. With exquisite brushwork and vibrant color, she transformed shells from the sea into cosmic cyclones and set flowers ablaze with sexuality. Her *Red Poppy*, painted in 1927, is pure Georgia—fiery, passionate, eternal.

"She used to say 'I'm going to live to be a hundred.' Then as she got closer to a hundred, she would say, 'Now I'm going to start. talking about living until a hundred and twenty,'" Juan Hamilton told me.

I'm at a dinner party sitting next to an artist named Jennifer Verklin, who just turned forty-two. She is a mixed-media oil painter, and I am talking to her about my fascination with Georgia O'Keeffe—her stamina, her ageless beauty. Verklin tells me that she wouldn't think twice about getting an eye lift or something else lifted or tightened as the years progress, but that she knows that looking different will not make her any more fulfilled.

"I am already happy," said Verklin. "I have work that I love. But if something really starts bothering me about how I look, I have no problem getting it fixed. I think of cosmetic surgery as an artistic method: I have a vision of myself, and if the physical package is deteriorating, I may need to do something to meet my own critical perception of myself. It's about keeping up with the vision of who you are. But looking good means nothing if you don't have a life that is good. And I have my art. I have my family. I have God."

Indeed, women and men who have fulfilling lives are the best candidates for plastic surgery because it's the frosting on the cake, it's not the whole cake. For me, my frosting is daily exercise, alternating between fast walks and weight-lifting sessions with my trainer, J. D., whose favorite line is "Give me ten more!" Aerobics and weights have given me a more defined body than I've ever had, and a sharper, better outlook; I spring out the door of the gym, muscles and senses primed, ready to burst through barriers. Ironically, exercising hard, when movement is all I am, provides an oasis of calm.

Aging can mean whatever you want it to mean; it certainly should not mean aspiring to look like a midlife actress whose physical perfection is from multiple cosmetic procedures, and is simply not attainable by the common woman. Start loving who you are at this moment, imperfections and flaws, whether you are thirty-eight or forty-six or sixty-four. You can run from your age, but ultimately you can't hide. My motto as I keep having birthdays every August is "Work on the neck down." Let our faces be formed by the elements and children and husbands who make us laugh and cry. And keep pumping the body and flexing the soul by being passionate and engaged in your life.

And from that place of synergy, if you opt for some surgical nips, you are a person who can handle it, knowing that a tighter face is not going to fix your life, because your life is already fixed. But beware to those of you contemplating a tad of Botox here and there. Once you start, it can be tough to stop there. Hear this story from Laurie, forty-one, about her initial consultation with one of the top plastic surgeons in the Southeast.

I have deep frown lines and a chin that hangs down, so I went to the doctor to see what he could do. He thought Botox would be great for the lines between my eyebrows and also for my left eyelid, which twitches. I then showed the doctor a picture of myself from a recent vacation which showed my sagging neck profile, and here's what happened next: After studying the picture, the doctor said that he thought a lower face-lift would be in order.

I asked him if we could just do liposuction on the fat below my chin, but he said at my age, the skin had lost too much elasticity for liposuction to work. Then he said, "While we're at it, we could do your eyes, too." I couldn't believe it! My first thought was: "Do what with my eyes?" I thought my eyes were fine; in fact they are one of my better physical assets. Finally, after we looked in the mirror together, he decided that the deep wrinkles on my forehead would best be removed by an upper face-lift. So here I am, thinking Botox when I came in, but by the end of my consultation I am needing an entire face-lift and eye job.

The next step was to do a computer image of what I would look like if the above procedures were done. So I went into a little room with an aesthetician, and while we were in there, I was visited by two staff members younger than me who showed me their surgically corrected faces. The results of the computer imaging were unbelievable! Eyebrows were raised, chicken chin was erased, wrinkles were removed, my nose was perfectly sculpted. Oh yeah, I forgot to mention that during the computer imaging, they also decided that I needed a nose job.

So what did I do? None of the above. I quickly saw that if I change one thing on my face, it changes everything, and I'd have to keep playing catch-up with added procedures. Then I'd have to get all that stuff done again and again when the wrinkles and flab inevitably return. You'll never be finished, and you'll never be satisfied. I'm only forty-one! I'm not willing to play this game for the next forty or fifty years of my life.

This is an extreme example, but it is not uncommon for people to get a minuscule procedure and then become hooked on the magic of having someone chisel out a new face. I know people who have had everything done and still feel like something is not quite right. Do what you have to do to uphold your vision of yourself. But don't let that vision get stuck in the trap of youth. Join me and other aging boomers who have lots of lines and lots of gray but still feel frisky and sexy and whole. Real beauty springs from an abiding joy.

I never want to look in the mirror and stare back at a stranger with orange highlights and a trampoline face who makes me shudder, "Oh my God! Who is that person?" I'll take the bad news now, that I'm no longer twenty-five, but hey, forty-seven feels great and I'm hell-bent on following in the footsteps of formidable mature women who celebrate their vintage. What Georgia O'Keeffe and Meryl Streep have to communicate about passion of the soul is far more interesting than reading how Britney Spears gets her belly so flat.

My mouth is slightly crooked and one eye slopes more than the other. I have a bump on the right side of my nose from the time I broke it on a bus going to camp in 1966, trying to do a back bend while straddling the aisle, standing on the armrests of two seats. I could get rid of the bump, but then I wouldn't think of Camp Agawak every time I touched it, and I love thinking about camp. We are all imperfect, flawed beings.

Yet when power and confidence lives in your heart, people won't be measuring you by what they see, but by the sheer weight of your being. You get a confident heart by giving life your all. You know the expression "She fills a room"? This isn't said about someone because of her size. A person who fills a room is a person with an expansive spirit, someone full of light, someone real.

When I look in the mirror I do love, more and more, this woman at midlife who is moving beyond her role as a mother of young children into something else exciting but uncertain. Self-love does not mean selfishness. By making the journey into self-acceptance, you can fully appreciate others. Know yourself before you start thinking about changing your face. What we need to seek is not a different body, but fitness of life.

A couple of years ago, a makeup artist was dolling me up before my appearance on a morning news program. She asked me if she could pluck my eyebrows, because "the eyebrows are *it* for a woman." She told me that a good eyebrow plucking could make me look like I just had a face-lift. Never having had a proper eyebrow shaping, I let her pluck away, watching in the mirror as my eyes widened and I seemed less tired. Like Nancy Reagan, I looked astonished. But in the car home from the studio, my brows were red and hurting, and I've never plucked like that again. Those skinny little arches weren't it for me. If the "eyebrows are it," we are all in trouble. Our infrastructures are it, not the glossy facades. Surgically induced astonishment doesn't last. Let's aim for soul-induced astonishment.

Mary Noble Ours is a portrait photographer in Washington, D.C., known for her ability to capture the true spirit of her subjects. I asked Ours about the Botox generation and about what she sees from behind her Hasselblad lens:

What is most appealing is a woman who shows expression, a woman who has a face full of life, rather than an expressionless face. I'm not opposed to Botox to soften frown lines that make you look angry, but you do not want to get rid of every line of expression. When people come to have their portrait done, many of them bring in an old picture of themselves and ask, "Can you make me look like this?" The picture may be twenty years old, of a completely unlined face. These are the people who are hesitant to smile for the camera because of all the crinkles around their eyes.

But if you don't smile, you're going to look vacant and joyless. One of my favorite photographs was done by Richard Avedon, a 1949 street scene in Paris called Dorian Leigh and Bicycle Racer. *And this woman is throwing her head back, laughing wildly, a huge smile, and her face is covered with expression lines, around her eyes, on her cheeks, everywhere. And she looks rapturous and beautiful. A face that is frozen is not attractive. I tell people that it is a myth if they think when they don't smile they will look younger.*

In fact, smiling picks up the face, and that is more youthful and jubilant than seeing a face devoid of emotion. Without a smile, the corners of the mouth sag downward, which really makes someone look older. I don't mind not seeing a woman's frown lines, which Botox can help. However, I am disappointed when a woman smiles and all the wrinkles around her eyes have been eradicated, so that her eyes don't get smaller, and the smile looks artificial. The mouth seems disconnected from the eyes. The fact is, when a person smiles, the eyes get smaller and the crinkles appear, and that can be beautiful.

From my vantage point, what counts as a woman ages is to have incredibly erect posture of the upper body. One of my biggest nags to my clients is to keep the chin level, so the light can fall more gracefully on the face. Poor posture, sagging shoulders, is what contributes to looking older. Standing straight shows strength and beauty at any age. So does a big smile, with crinkles; it lights up everything, it shows a person at ease in life.

SURRENDERING TO YOURSELF

SELF BEYOND MARRIAGE

Bob Dylan is singing "Don't Think Twice" to me on my car stereo, his crackly voice sharing something we've all felt about an ex, how he gave her his heart, but she wanted his soul. And he's got me thinking about how much we pour into love. We give relationships our dreams, our hearts, bits of our souls. Too often we are devastated when they give us less back. After talking to three hundred husbands and wives and lovers in various stages of relationships for *Surrendering to Marriage*, I know that much of the malaise in love comes from expecting someone else to make you happy and complete, to be a match of the soul. There isn't a person alive who can do that; only you can make yourself happy, only you complete your self.

This concept our generation has promoted of finding your soul mate and not settling for less does more damage than good to the stability of a marriage. The person who snores next to you and with whom you share a bathroom may not feel like as much of a soul mate as the man at work you have a crush on who hangs on your every word, thinks you are gorgeous, and takes your breath away. But try living with Mr. Hubba-Hubba from the office, and he'll become Mr. Ho-Hum real fast.

Here's what I'm finding after nearly fifteen years of matrimony. I am indeed my own soul mate and you are your own soul mate, and the mating of the soul happens in ourselves. My husband and I share love, lust, commitment, a house, children, in-laws, bills. But we do not share one soul. We are two souls who dance, who dodge, who meld, who repel. He is my husband and I am his wife, but I cannot give him my whole heart and soul. What I do give him, however, is heartfelt and soulful. You can be successful at being in love only after you learn to love who you are when you are *not* in love, the you in aloneness. Our lovers must not define us.

I shudder at some of the forms love has taken in my past, having felt sometimes like Shakespeare's Cleopatra as she anticipates being away from Antony: "Give me to drink mandragora, that I might sleep out the great gap of time/my Antony is away." The besotted Cleopatra cannot bear to be conscious while they are apart, so great is the pain of solitude. Like a parasite, she is clinging to her lover, to how he makes her feel.

Cleopatra's brand of love, offering everything and expecting everything, leads only to heartache. But when you pour yourself into your own life—creating, contributing, unleashing your passions, helping others discover theirs—you will never be disappointed. You are your own soul mate, so the hunt for a perfect match to fill that gap can stop. You are the loved one you should be searching to fully know; you are the only loved one capable of coming through for yourself time and time again. Then you can love fully, when you fully love yourself.

Many people tell me they would like to try marriage therapy but can't get their spouses to go. And I recommend that they go by themselves. Go talk about what makes them so angry about their husbands or wives. Find out what they think they need to change about their partners to make themselves happy. Look at what's missing from their own lives.

Usually we discover that discontent had very little to do with the other people and everything to do with us. What are you doing for yourself to streamline your anger and enhance your joy? What is your artery of life outside of your marriage? If you don't have one, you'd better get one, and I don't mean other romantic interests. I'm talking about work or a hobby that fills you and propels you, a passion that stretches your humanness. Often our complaints about marriage have to do with a perceived stagnancy in the relationship, when it's really a stagnant self that needs to get moving.

Let me save you the fees and agony of divorce if you're simply bored with your spouse, and not in an abusive or otherwise battering marriage: Take on a mission that makes you leap out of bed in the morning, and see how much better your marriage and your self can become. About five years ago I felt stuck in my writing—overwhelmed by young children; too weary to be inspired; creatively taut, not loose like an artist needs to be. I went two months without touching my computer, couldn't go near the thing. I had nothing new to say. Needless to say, I was not the most chipper and nurturing of wives during this dark period, when I felt disconnected from my self. One Saturday a friend asked Chuck and me to go out on his speedboat, and as we whipped through the balmy May air I noticed a pair of green water skis on the floor. I asked our friend, also named Chuck, if he would pull me in the boat on those skis, explaining that I had not been waterskiing in twenty-five years and could use a boost right now.

I lowered myself into the Severn River, slipped my feet into the black rubber shoes on the skis, grabbed the tow rope between my knees in ready position, following the drill as if I had just skied yesterday. The boat accelerated, and I got right up and stayed up during the entire five-minute ride, even while crashing in and out of the wakes. When I finally let go of the rope and signaled to the guys that I had enough, I was screaming, "I did it! I did it!" in a rush of childlike zeal. A hard shell cracked that day, and my fluid soul, imprisoned temporarily, was released, and I started writing again, hard and well. When my computer and I are friends, my marriage is on a far better track.

I am looking at a picture I keep on my desk of Chuck and me, taken a couple of weeks after we met, in October 1985. We are climbing the rocks in Harpers Ferry, West Virginia, a town where two rivers, the Potomac and the Shenandoah, meet, and where three states—West Virginia, Maryland, and Virginia—come together. When this new Chuck, whom I liked deeply and immediately, asked me to spend the day with him in Harpers Ferry, I thought this was a good omen, that he would plan an outing to this town known for its confluence of states and waterways, where perhaps we too were meant to flow together as one.

When he picked me up at my Washington apartment early that morning, I let out a small gasp when I saw what he was wearing, which was the same thing I was wearing; a V-neck white T-shirt and baggy khakis. There was an ancient familiarity about this man at my door, the one in rumpled garb with curly hair.

Today, as I'm looking at the picture of us in white T-shirts against the jagged gray rocks I know he is my soul mate and I know he is not. Yes, because we met and mated and created four creatures who are a mosaic of our love and genes. No, because although we are one organism now, the Anthony tribe, I am one soul, and they are their own souls. The missing pieces that we search for in other people when we are young are really within us, although we don't know it at the time. For me, it took writing about the challenges of marriage and feeling my way around my own mercurial marriage to understand what it takes to make a relationship last, and that is a passion of the soul beyond each other. This is great news because it frees you to quit expecting another person to fill your deepest needs, to complete your unfinished business. What would you do if he died?

Natalie was thirty-five and eight months pregnant, married to "my first incredible love," a man with whom she operated a large manufacturer of designer accessories. While Natalie and Charlie were driving home on a Saturday afternoon, after eighteen holes of golf, a drunk driver swerved into their Jeep on the ramp leading onto the expressway. Her husband, Charlie, a vigorous triathlete, was at the wheel and died soon after the accident. Natalie broke bones and lost consciousness but carried the baby for the full nine months, a girl born healthy. Here is Natalie's story of getting on with her life after experiencing the worst event imaginable:

We had our first date in March, and we were married that August in Kennebunkport, Maine, where my family has a house. I was twenty-four, he was thirty, and we were madly in love. We had a very tough time getting pregnant. It took five years, four different doctors, lots of tests, surgery for Charlie and multiple surgeries for me. We swung through major lows together. Ironically, he never got to meet that child we worked so hard to have. It is truly sad because it was Charlie's optimism, his encouragement, that carried me through.

We bought a new puppy to grow up with the baby, and Charlie would walk around holding the puppy, telling everyone he was practicing holding the baby. The baby gift he loved most was from his best friend, who gave him a roll of duct tape for the diaper changing. Charlie used duct tape for everything! I had the baby six weeks after he died. His last words to the shock trauma unit were, "I'm okay, take care of Natalie and the baby." With everything I went through, the pain of losing him—I lost my teeth, broke my pelvis, had a concussion where I temporarily lost most of my sight—this baby not only survived the accident, she went term. She was meant to be here. I didn't get my full eyesight back until after she was born.

It was incredible when she was born and I first saw her. She looked exactly like her father. Charlie was back. That was my gift from my husband. After only eleven years of marriage, I had a whole new life I needed to start. There I was, a thirty-five-year-old widow, alone with a newborn. How could this happen to me? Everything was so perfect. Our marriage was magnificent. He was my friend, my husband, my sports partner, my business partner. My storybook life was destroyed.

Soon after, my father was diagnosed with a terminal illness. My older brother was going through a divorce. So there I was six weeks after my baby's birth, celebrating Christmas at my parents' home, with no husband and a baby; my brother was there alone without his sons and his wife, and my dad is ill. Christmas morning, I noticed my Dad was missing. My mom found him in their bedroom crying from a broken heart over his children. My father's health took a serious turn for the worse, and he died a year later.

I have kept all the letters from people describing Charlie and our marriage for our daughter to read when she is ready. It was phenomenal; we had the kind of easy and natural relationship that most people strive to have for their whole lives. After he was killed, I remember lying on the bed in such physical pain next to my mom and crying my heart out, just crying and crying in agony. I didn't know anyone my age I could talk to about this; women my age were just starting their families, they were not in mourning.

I kept going over the moment of death, over the whole scenario. I would think: If I hadn't gone to the bathroom before we got into the car, we wouldn't have been at that place at that time. I fell asleep right before the crash, and I remember my last words to Charlie. We were on the express-way getting on a ramp, and there had been new construction on the road. There were these huge new concrete pilings as we entered the ramp, and I said, "I wonder what that's going to be for?" With that, I fell asleep, and never spoke to my husband again.

My last memory of being with Charlie were the lights of emergency vehicles. I woke up in a shock trauma unit very confused and in tremendous pain, and my oldest brother was there. I said to my brother: "What happened?" He told me that there was an accident and I said, "Well, where's Charlie? Go find Charlie." And I pushed him away and went back to sleep. I have no idea how much longer it was when my brother came back with the doctor, who told me my husband had died. It was horrifying. I didn't believe him. I looked at my brother, the pain in my body now excruciating. It was as if my heart was wrenched from me.

I lived and he died. I believe I was saved because I hadn't done my work here yet. Charlie had already touched so many lives. Almost immediately after, I went looking for a white-picket-fence life again, and made the mistake of getting married quickly. The relationship was abusive and very brief. Unlike my first marriage, I got pregnant right away, and I do have a wonderful son from that marriage. Then a few years ago, I married again, and this was another big mistake. We recently divorced.

Today, I can say how truly grateful I am for the life I have. I am very excited about who my children are becoming. My twenty-five-year-old company has survived all my ups and downs and is still my passion and is thriving. I started my business from scratch in 1977, and today our products are sold in five hundred retail stores nationwide, from Bloomingdale's and Neiman-Marcus to dozens of boutiques. After Charlie died, this company was my anchor. The business is still a great passion, but it is not my anchor. My true anchor is in my heart and soul.

It will be thirteen years this summer since he is gone, and at first the loneliness was all encompassing. I would have a glass of wine to make me happy and a glass to drown my sorrow. I remember being down in my basement ironing, drinking, and my children asleep upstairs, and I'm thinking, "I am miserable, what am I going to do?" Charlie and I had a friend in Alcoholics Anonymous and I went to talk to him. Quickly my thoughts turned to "Wait a minute. I've got a family. I have a business. I'm healthy. I can't drink like this."

At the age of forty-eight, I have really been around many bends on a very long road. My mother died a year ago, so now I am totally on my own, and that has been a real awakening. My mother and I talked at least once a week on the phone, I'm the only girl in the family, with two brothers, so we were very close. She was tough on me and had great expectations, but to lose your mother is to lose your lifeline. So I know now, "Okay, Natalie, it's really time to grow up."

Yet I do not feel lonely, even though there are many times I feel like picking up the telephone and calling my mother. I wish she could see how much I have finally grown up, how self-sufficient I've become. But then I say to myself, "She sees me, she's here." It's the same way I feel about Charlie. He is definitely here. I pray a lot to them, my dad too, for advice or just wanting to share news with them. They are very much alive in my soul. I was with my husband for eleven years, and I had my mother for forty-seven years, and you just can't be with people for that length of time and have it be over. It is never over. They are all parked in little corners of my heart.

I can't say there is something I don't have that I want. I'm on the right road. Yet, September 11 reopened a lot of wounds for me, all the young women who lost husbands, it was unreal how fresh it made Charlie's death in my mind. If you had a wonderful relationship, you want one again, very, very badly. After Charlie died, I poured myself into my work, and despite my rockiness at the time, the business survived and really started growing. Charlie and I were going to sell the business and raise our kids in Colorado, but after the accident, I couldn't do that. My business was my anchor.

I've come to know that no man or no business is really your anchor. I am anchored in myself. I was so wobbly for so long with all that had happened to me, but recently I woke up and said, "You know, Natalie, you're more than okay. You're doing better than you've ever done in your life." I was close, but I didn't hit rock bottom. And I realized that you are the most important anchor you've got. The anchor is within, and if you don't know it and feel it now, figure out how to get it there.

I would also tell people to spend as much time as you can

with friends and family who are very ill or dying. I did have a chance with my father and found joy out of being with him during his slow and painful death. He used to love to eat, and when I would visit, I would always cook some of his favorite things. As his illness took over, he lost his appetite, and I would make that my challenge. I would figure out the tastiest, most tender things and he would just love it. It meant everything to me to be able to give happiness to someone near his death, because I never got to do that for Charlie.

I am proud of who I have become. I have survived a lot and accomplished a lot. After Charlie's death, I felt like I had no roots. Yes, it took a lot of time to get that monkey off my back and to be standing on my own two feet. There's a maturity now, as I approach fifty, that is unprecedented in my life, a deeper love and appreciation for my children and my friends, a deeper spirituality and a true love for myself.

Hearing Natalie, I think of Henry David Thoreau, who retreated alone into the woods of Walden to "live deliberately," as he described it, to savor his solitude, in nature, away from people, to taste what he called the "marrow of existence." Our own deliberate life cannot be wired for us by another person. We must choose how we fill our days; led by the spirit within, we must excavate our own marrow-deep self. Partners bolster us; we cry on their shoulders; they give us intimacy and companionship and love. But it is dangerous to count on someone else to put meaning, marrow, into your life.

Rifling through pages of my diaries, I read passages that make me groan, sentences that make me thankful that I am no longer looking for love in all the wrong places, but looking to myself. On May 3, 1979, at the age of twenty-five, this is my recording after a break-up with a Chicago bartender who was so handsome and so bad I cried nearly every day of our six-month relationship: "I know it's good that this guy is gone, but he took a hunk of my heart with him. And now comes loneliness, the sheer terror of coming home to my apartment to no phone calls, no plans, to nobody."

Sheer terror from being alone is not something anybody should ever feel, and I'd like to save you from that desperate ache by telling you this: Whoever you are with right now is someone you may love deeply and depend on for many things. But you can live without this person; he or she does not give you your breath, your talents, your dreams. Alone-ness must never cause terror, or else you are doomed to spend many years of your life terrorized. Loved ones leave. Loved ones die. These facts are brutal but inevitable. So get strong now. Realize that what you possess is unshakable, indomitable, mighty, an inner core that no other person can promise, or give you. So relax in love; the other person doesn't have the goods to make you happy. You have the goods.

I'm singing "You Make Me Feel Like a Natural Woman" loudly in the shower while massaging shampoo into my hair. These lyrics have always made my heart race, for different reasons, depending on which era of my life I have sung them. This song of love popularized by Aretha Franklin speaks of life being "unkind" until the right man comes along and gives "peace of mind," a sentiment many of us have felt. In classic Aretha, seductive and piercing, she goes on to sing of feeling like her soul is in the lost-and-found, until "you came along to claim it," at which time, the lovelorn woman feels fully alive, like a natural woman.

I'm feeling like a natural but cranky woman, stuck in a long security-checkpoint line with a hassled husband and four tired kids at Baltimore-Washington International Airport right around Valentine's Day. I get to talking to an exotic young woman with vexing cat eyes who tells me she writes poetry about life and love. We exchange cards; her real name is Deborah Grison, pen name Collage. A few days later I get a package with a slim volume of poetry called *the attic*, and flicking through the pages I stop on "My Soul's Ideal Mate." As you can tell from these verses, Collage writes openly of searching for her "perfect man." In the meantime, she is working hard on herself, studying for a Ph.D. in urban and regional planning and writing poetry, "so that when I am found I too can be someone's ideal mate," she says.

Blacker than the darkest night and hotter than 10,000
coals.
Stronger than 1 million men that possess the deepest
souls

Loving like the Swallows of Capistrano when they mate
As intuitive as a Psychic Friend, for he always knows
*   his fate.*
Will cook, and bring me breakfast
with a yellow rose in bed.
Hears my thoughts before I speak them,
for he knows what's going on in my head.
Intelligent as Einstein, Imhoptep, and a child prodigy.
Reads everything he can find,
but is partial to those things spiritual, and books that
record our history.
Knows his purpose in this world;
he's my diamond in the rough,
and I am his cultured pearl
See, the man I just described is my ideal mate.
We haven't met one another yet, but
it is our destiny, our fate.

I call Collage and tell her, "Come on, this guy is a fantasy. You will never get it all." Then I dangle the notion in front of her that what she is looking for is already in herself, that she is her own soul mate. Single and twenty-nine, Collage says she is already whole in the Lord, but still unabashedly calls herself a "lady in waiting," for a companion, for children, for the completion of the wife-mother destiny she believes is hers to have. Hearing her dreams, I realize that it wasn't until I was well into marriage and childbearing that I became solid and secure enough to meet myself as my own soul mate. It wasn't until this moment, really. Without the foundation of a family, I too would likely be writing poetry to someone who will find me, like these words by Collage:

Ask and ye shall receive
and be patient for what the Lord has planned,
and soon, I believe, I will be found by my perfect man.

Indeed, the prospect is alluring to be found by someone who loves you unequivocally and wants you forever. And when love strikes, that person often does seem perfect– nothing beats the breathless infatuation of a steamy new union. But beware when someone else makes you feel stronger, smarter, and more beautiful than you have ever felt before. Because when he or she vanishes, so goes your invincibility. The one line of "You Make Me Feel Like a Natural Woman" on a woman's soul in the lost-and-found rips through me every time, because I have felt that way and hated feeling that way, waiting for someone to claim me. Long ago, in a relationship more crazy than anything I've ever experienced, I let someone claim my soul and he let me claim his soul, and I was him and he was me, and I didn't eat, I didn't sleep, I was a woman stricken by love. Then the loving stopped, and so did my world for a while, and I will never again let anyone move into me that way, and take over.

We can't allow our power to be gotten from the adoration of someone else—real power stems from the beams in our soul, a soul we own and no one else gets to claim. We make us feel like natural women and men by loving our natural selves.

It's 4:06 A.M. at a hotel near the Grand Canyon where we are vacationing, the day before Easter in 2002. And I am shaken out of a thick sleep by a weird dream, in which my husband has agreed to join a string quartet of stunning women—and move to another state. I wake up with a jolt and am compelled to shake him and tell him my dream must mean something. What does it mean? I inhale deeply, and instead of rousing him so he can assure me that he loves only me, I get out of bed, grab my journal, and go into the bathroom.

Sitting on the cold terra-cotta floor, I write: "Chuck can tell me he loves me, but I must reach inward for reaffirmation, and you know, as I get older and smarter about love, it's starting to work nearly every time."

The more we can do that in life, feel loved without someone saying "I love you," the better off we are. I have me, you have you, we have our spiritual links, we have our soul's work. I am an officer of our temple and part of my duties are to assist the rabbi and cantor once a month with Friday night and Sabbath services. At bar and bat mitzvahs, I get to present the boy or girl with a personally inscribed Talmud, the ancient book of our people. At the ceremony for one boy named Matthew, I told him: "As you turn thirteen and become a bar mitzvah, I can tell you that people and things will come and go in your life, but you will always have your Judaism. No one can ever take that away from you." What a comfort it has been for me to know that I own a heritage that is centuries old. What a gift to have God, an almighty ally throughout everything.

As the years of marriage roll on, to an extraordinary man who loves his family unfailingly, I am increasingly aware that love is splendid and sex is energizing, but that our partners alone cannot feed our hungry souls. That's our task, our responsibility, and expecting someone else to do it for us is a ticket to divorce. Unfortunately it can take a bull-dozing experience to get people to start looking for love in all the right places. Walking on the trail this morning I passed a neighbor, a woman of fifty-one who is one year past a bad split with a husband who left her for another woman. She was walking fast, in short shorts, head erect, arms swinging, self-possessed. A year ago, she was hunched over and glum, yearning for the man who walked out after twenty-three years of marriage and who wasn't walking back in. Her pain was searing; it was impossible to talk to her without feeling an arrow in your own heart.

She says that his swift and unexpected departure forced her to get rid of her old self and become someone new, and that self is heartier and more authentic than the one who was supplicant, under his thumb, "worried about what he would think." Don't make a spouse the centerpiece of your life; your soul and spirit are the only things you can't live without. Worry about what *you* think.

Suzi was the It-girl growing up in Menlo Park, California. She was the best female athlete in her class, had the most desirable boyfriends. Everyone wanted to be her friend. The child of blue-collar parents, she studied briefly at the community college, then went to work as a waitress in nearby Palo Alto at a popular oasis for Stanford students. It was there that she met a "drop-dead handsome" sophomore named Brad, a star athlete she married at twenty-three, had three children with, and who transported her into another sphere, into a big house, with plenty of money.

To friends and family, Suzi and Brad seemed like the ideal match. They complemented each other's good looks and lived in a splendid home; their kids were polite and did well in school. To keep up her image, Suzi never let on that in her house of gold, Brad was never around, that he played as hard as he worked, and that she felt more lonely than loved. "I didn't trust him as far as I could throw him," she says.

Here's how it feels for Suzi to have put twenty-one years of eggs in someone else's basket, then to pick herself up and shift her trust into the sturdy basket of self:

"It's My Turn" by Diana Ross really speaks to me at this point in my life. Because I've lived much of my life through the eyes of other people and for other people. I've put them first.

Even as a child, I was out to please other people. I was one of six children, and my family came first. Then my husband and children came first. Even though I'm the second in the line of six, I was the oldest daughter, and there was a seven-year span between the first three kids and the second three, and I was the one who parented my younger siblings.

My father worked in a factory and my mother took ill when I was very young with a thyroid condition. So I was a daughter, then a mother, then a wife, and my sense of self came from my duties in life trying to serve other people. I come from a strong Catholic background and grew up right across the street from a convent. It was instilled in me from my earliest memory that life was to be lived for others.

So that's what I did. In high school, I always had two different types of friends, so I wouldn't have to become one type of person or another. And maybe I wasn't sure where I really belonged. The first set were risk takers, always testing authority. Then there were my cheerleader friends, model students, model citizens. The two groups were rivals and I was the bridge between both groups. I enjoyed wearing both hats.

From my teens, I always had a boyfriend. My parents had a good marriage and it seemed right to have someone of the opposite sex in my life. Although I was having a lot of fun, it was a confusing time, very social, not as academic as it should have been. I very much wanted to go into the medical field. I wanted to be a nurse or a doctor, and I didn't have the grades to get into college for that. So I became lost.

Instead of becoming serious about college, I waitressed at a place where I met all kinds of college students, and that's where I met my husband. He walked in one night and I served him a burger, medium rare, and he flirted and I flirted. He was very sure of himself. Very good-looking. He was a sophomore in college, and he played football and baseball. He was a real star.

We got along immediately. We were both quick-witted. We both gave the impression that we were very confident. Looking back on everything, our confidence levels were really a different story. A year after he graduated from college, we got married. I was twenty-three, and it was 1977.

I got pregnant right away, then had our son in 1978. It was everything I always dreamed of. I wanted to have a family, I wanted to be a mother. I wanted no part of the working woman scene. My husband got into the real estate business, and we survived on very little income for the early years of our marriage. In order to make ends meet I worked part-time as a Kelly girl and in winter heated only the kitchen and bedroom of our five-room apartment. Even though it was not where we ultimately wanted to be, I felt that we were on the right track.

There was conflict early in our marriage, which came from my husband spending very little time at home. He worked very, very hard, but he also played very, very hard, not only golf, but everything. This was unacceptable to me. We ended up staying married for twenty-one years and having three children together; the last baby just started college; the first baby is graduating from college this year.

In the mid-eighties, my husband started to become more successful, becoming part owner of a large real estate company. And in many ways, I continued to have a dream life. As his business grew, we attained all the material goods we could possibly want. We moved into a big house and had a membership at the country club. We both drove luxury automobiles and I loved the winter so I could wear my mink coat. I think he liked me wearing it more than I did, for the image it portrayed. But it was a picket-fence surface dream that camou-

flaged a marriage that was coming apart. I just didn't want the world to see I had failed, I guess, so I did everything to keep the picture pretty.

My children were horrified with the news that their parents were separating. They were shocked. Everybody who knew us was shocked. I was shocked that he actually left the house, because my sense of family is paramount. You stay married, period. It was like you fix what's broken, you don't leave it.

But my husband and I had been on a parallel trip in our lives throughout this last fifteen years, where I was home raising the children and he was out climbing the corporate ladder. I knew he had to build his business, yet I felt that even though we were going this parallel road we would eventually meet somewhere along the way in our two lives. But our two lives were very separate; we were living together physically but living very far apart emotionally. At some point you have to intertwine, and we did not.

During the separation, I was very conscious about what other people would think. I fought very hard to save the marriage. I did everything in my power for this not to happen. We were separated four years before the actual divorce. I was totally broken when he left. His game was that he kept pulling me back and I would go back. He wouldn't let me go completely, so I never quite believed our marriage would actually end. I thought he was just going through a phase, a midlife crisis. I thought that he needed his space, he needed to find himself—that's what he told the children—indicating that he might come back. Again, my thoughts were on him and his growth, and not me and my growth.

He had the power, absolutely, and this went on for quite a while. My sense of self was terrible during this time; it was nonexistent. I was living for my children, I was living for him, I was trying to fix him, and not working at all at trying to fix or resurrect myself.

But over the years, I have started to believe in myself, and that has been the most difficult thing to do. Trust my instincts, finally believe that what has happened to my marriage wasn't all my fault. I blamed myself for the breakup; I used to tell my therapist: "I am the reason he's gone." When it finally clicked that he *is the reason he's gone, not me, a whole different dynamic starting happening with me. That's when I started the "it's my turn" attitude. And looking back at our marriage, I saw a lot of places it wasn't such a dream life that I was leaving behind. He was not loyal in our marriage. He was always late. He was not dependable. Why was I trying to hold on to this?*

I tried for too long to keep up a good image for my parents, siblings, and friends, wearing any hat I needed to wear so we could uphold the picture of a happy family. I particularly needed to keep up a good front for my mother. She lived vicariously through me; she thought my husband was the be-all and end-all. I was raised in a very modest household, with just the bare necessities—food, shelter, clothing. My husband gave me and my children everything materially we ever asked for, and she thought that was the ultimate for a husband to do. When I told her on the telephone that he was leaving, her first reaction was one of embarrassment. She was humiliated.

What would she tell her friends? She still refers to the divorce as "what he did to us."

Throughout much of our separation, my husband would come to the house freely any time he wanted. It was an open-door policy. I tried to set boundaries, but he is a man who lives with no boundaries. One day I heard my fourteen-year-old daughter talking to him from her bedroom window: "Dad, I don't think it's right that you come here any time you want to. You should call first." So he left, feeling rejected. The next time he came, he called first. That night he took our daughter out to dinner. He told her that she had no idea how much he sacrificed for her, then asked why she was treating him like this. And she said, "Well, Dad, I thought parents were supposed to sacrifice for their kids, not the other way around."

When she told me this, I asked her: "Jill, where did you ever get an idea like that?" And she said, "Mom, I got it from you. You are always doing things for us." I was surprised to hear her say that. I was also bursting with pride and I began to laugh and cry all at once. She was able to get him to respond in a way that I was never able to. My kids, my baby, perceived me as this person who was strong. From that point on, I started setting boundaries on him. Our home was no longer the Do Drop Inn. It was my house with my set of rules, not his. This new attitude felt very gratifying. It gave me the confidence to make my own decisions and feel good about them. It was as though my daughter showed me that I needed to do what I felt was right. And I started doing something else I had never done before: I started to allow myself to be vulnerable. I took off the "I am okay" mask that I was wearing for every-body else.

Throughout all this, if people asked me if I was hurting, I would say, "I'm okay." I realized that I needed to tell the truth about when I was hurting. I was being the caregiver all the time, the mother and the wife and the friend everyone came to. And I would never go to anybody when I needed help. And so in many ways I was living a lie. The fake Suzi can do anything. The real Suzi is someone no one knew and I was afraid to show, even in my marriage. Therapy was a turning point for me.

I had been totally obsessed with my husband and what was wrong with him. Why didn't he want to be with me? Why didn't he want to be married to me? My therapist said, "Let's not bring him into our session, Suzi. This is not about him. This is about you." She made it clear to me that this was not couples therapy since, after all, I was the only one there. She forced me to focus on me.

My self-esteem grew slowly but surely. We were separated for almost four years by now. I was sure he would never, ever change, and at this point I didn't care if he did or not. It took me quite a while to trust again in relationships, and it was a conscious effort on my part not to be attracted to the type of guy I had always been attracted to my whole life—handsome, gregarious, the bad boy you couldn't quite get your hands on. So I opened up my mind to all different scenarios, and I actu-ally ended up going on-line to a dating website. That's where I met the wonderful man I am living with now.

Meeting a person on-line was a good thing for me. I first

got to know him from the inside out, not from the outside in. On-line, you are not dazzled by how someone looks or acts. They are writing you and you get to know what's in their heart. As a matter of fact, if I had first seen this man at a bar or night-club, I don't think I would have given him a second look. But this man is trustworthy, kind, and considerate. He is honest, loyal, responsible, and always on time. There is no doubt in my mind that he is totally there for me. What a great feeling that has been. We're best friends and lovers.

Most important, I am there for me. The me in this relationship is very different than the me in my marriage. It's not a needy me. I will now accept someone caring for me or helping me when I need it, as opposed to trying to act strong and do it all myself so the world will think I'm perfect. I've given up the all-powerful Suzi. I am willing to cry and have a little self-pity party for myself every once in a while. It was very difficult for me to admit to people that I am vulnerable after years of wearing this mask.

In her song, Diana Ross sings: "It's my turn with no more room for lies. For years I've lived my life through someone else's eyes." The mask is off and the real Suzi has been exposed. The sunlight is making me thrive, not wilt. It really is my turn to live my life as I see fit to live it.

DISCARDING OLD SELVES

Shedding an old self and birthing a new self like Suzi did starts by getting rid of everything in your life that doesn't feel right. That means discarding people, jobs, obsessions, habits. Recently I had a large splinter embedded in the palm of my hand, and it stayed there for a couple of days because I knew that rooting it out would require lengthy pin-pricking, and that would hurt. When the site became inflamed, I had to get it out. So on a sunny morning, sitting on the rim of my bathtub by the window, I ran the tips of my Tweezermans and a sewing needle through a flame to sterilize them and started surgery. It took a long time and the pierces burned but I pulled the sliver out, in one piece, with one yank, leaving a clean wound that healed quickly.

Plucking a shaving of wood from my hand reminded me that along with surface splinters, we can root out pieces of ourselves that are embedded not in flesh but in our characters, old memories that make us feel guilty or sad, quirks that get us in trouble, relationships that won't leave us even though the person split long ago. Discarding old selves is a necessary step in unleashing, and surrendering to, your original spirit. One self I discarded, with a loud "good riddance," is the one who was spinning so fast she was missing out on her life, the woman who had trouble concentrating on the taste of her food because her mind was absorbed in plotting her next move. About two years ago, I was eating lump crabmeat, fresh and succulent, from the nearby bay. I love crab, immensely. At one point—I have no idea how much time had gone by, but I looked at my plate and it was clean except for a smear of tartar sauce. And I got so sad: Here I just downed one of my favorite meals and I had no recollection of its sweetness, the texture, the unfettered joy I get from eating crab on a hot summer night.

I still move fast, but I am better at knowing when I need to take my foot off the pedal, get out of my head and into the moment. At meals I am now conscious to be fully where I am, to chew slowly and enjoy each bite. Eating has actually become meditative for me. Even when I'm thick in a deadline, I refuse to slam down lunch, hunched over my computer. I take a twenty-minute break and sit at my kitchen table where I can see the river and the trees and have a real meal, usually a bountiful salad, and try to clear my mind of everything but the sharpness of the cheddar and the creaminess of the avocado and the nutty cilantro.

It is possible to dispose of parts of yourself you simply don't want to own anymore. You do not have to hold remorse in your heart forever, or other acidic emotions that eat you alive. You can free yourself from yourself. Therapy helps stir things up, but it is ultimately you who must give yourself permission to let go of vintage waste that is dragging you down and holding you back. It is up to you to dig deep, however excruciating is the act of cleaning out your life. For me that means working at loosening my attachment to my father; although he has been gone for sixteen years, his grip on me has only recently eased. He was everything to me for thirty-one years, the age I was when he died—my primary emotional support, the person who guided my career, the smart and funny person who thought I was so smart and funny I started believing it myself. No one could measure up to this incomparable role model and cheerleader. I went to my dad for all my big decisions; he was the only person I listened to, I would always do what he advised. Then, suddenly he was gone, and I was here, a shell, lost.

It took many grieving years to grow to a place where I could see that although a daughter never gets from anyone else what she gets from a kind and attentive father, this daughter would be fine. He gave me a great start, and the rest was up to me.

In order to get at the splinter in my hand, I had to prick through several layers of skin with a thin, sharp needle. My eyes were tearing and my palm was on fire. But I kept going, slowly, directed, intent on not quitting until I got the thing out. Last summer, I had another memorable splinter at camp, a speck of pine in the fleshy part of the base of my thumb. I went a full two weeks before doing anything about it. Finally I went at it, but the procedure hurt so much I stopped and left part of it in. When the hole healed over, the splinter site was more red then before I began. Finally I bit my lip, got out the needle, and burrowed it out, all of it, which I should have done the first time, and endured the pain. Just like real splinters, we should get at our slivers in the soul when they start to haunt us rather than wait for them to fester and worsen.

I am working along with you on discarding selves that are impediments, the impatient self who needs to sit more than run, and keeping the ones that have done me right, such as the teenage self who is very bold and slightly naughty. The spirit of youth is not something anyone should delete. Remember who you were in third grade, in seventh grade, your senior year in high school, as a newlywed, the day you brought your first child home from the hospital. If you don't have diaries to assist your memories, ask old friends and family elders what they remember. It is important to get a panoramic view of the swooping landscape of your life, to figure out what parts you want to chuck, what parts you want to hold on to, what parts you lost and want to get back. What I notice in my journals is that many core components of self have never wavered: I've always been quick, tenacious, and ambitious.

This is good and this is bad. Good, because I go after what I want, and keep trying even if I fail the first or second or third time out, if I know it's right for me. These can be bad traits as well, because moving quickly means missing out on some of the extraordinary subtleties in ordinary life, the magic that blooms in moments of repose. At forty-seven, I am working hard at learning how to shift my foot to the brake more often, to replenish the reservoirs I drain by moving so fast. I try now to keep the languor of summer in my soul all year round, to do absolutely nothing sometimes, to succumb to marvelous lethargy.

Years ago in my hometown of Chicago I knew a restaurateur named Sam who owned a beer garden. Sam always wore white jeans and Hawaiian shirts and bay rum splash tinged with lime, in June, in November, throughout the Windy City's arctic freeze. While other Chicago restaurants were serving up leaden winter stews, Sam featured huge salads and fresh fish in fruit marinades. At fifty, he would start his day by running ten miles along the Chicago lakefront in the most frigid of months, glowing like a high school athlete. External forces never toppled this man; he was light and fluid and on fire, moment to moment.

Holding on to the soul of summer means, no matter how busy we are, we must leave time for relaxation, which binds us to our essence. When we become still and stop whirring through time, we notice clouds that look like iridescent wax puffs and hummingbirds on the black-eyed Susans. We feel our breath, our God, who we really are.

We've all heard too many stories from workaholic parents, with kids entering college, who are now lamenting that they should have, wish they had, spent more time at home with a family that is now out the door for good. We've heard too many stories from husbands married to breast cancer survivors, and wives married to prostate cancer survivors, who had to have disaster strike before they realized with a jolt what wonderful people they are married to. What are you hankering to do today that you haven't done for a while because your life has been too crazy? Do it, and then do more of it. Those of us in professions that push us to our physical or emotional limits need to pay attention to replenishing our inner reserves.

In excavating my own self and drawing intimate stories from others for this book, there were plenty of days when I couldn't think anymore, couldn't feel anymore. It was a weariness that felt threatening not just to my body: my soul, too, was flattened. On many days I was in bed by 7:30 P.M., flopping onto the red flannel comforter, staring at the hypnotic flicker of headlights on the bridge in the distance until I conked out. One night I dreamt of marshmallows, flaming first, then amber and gooey, a cycle of eating and roasting and eating and roasting. For some reason, after the marshmallow dream I snapped out of my weariness and my engine was back running, all cylinders fired.

On the Severn River at dawn, mist rises and the sky is pink and I get to be alone in my kitchen, the red tile floor cold on my feet. Often there are lone kayakers on the still waters, oars held upward like spears. By 6:00 A.M., the trail of cars thickens on the bridge, commuters from the Eastern Shore of Maryland streaming across the Chesapeake Bay into Washington, an hour and a half away. I am happy not to be in a stiff suit and air-conditioned car this warm fall morning. I am relieved to be in gray drawstring pants and a yellow T-shirt printed with a blue map of Corfu, the outfit I slept in and will stay in all day. I am sorry for those people in their cars listening to the news and talking on cell phones—people who wish they were still on their porches, gazing across backyard creeks with willowy grasses that are everywhere in our region, finishing their cups of coffee that they had to leave in a hurry, half full, now cold.

I am aware that most people cannot linger on porches because they are due at offices that require a commute in traffic. It is a luxury to work at home, in sloppy clothes. But everyone, the poorest, the busiest, the most single-minded workhorse, needs to take a personal Sabbath, even if it's only for an hour a day, to listen to Handel after everyone else is asleep. Without snippets of leisure, we dry up inside. When your tank is empty, like mine was the week of the marshmallow dream, and you hit a wall, let the impact be incentive to remove yourself from the grind and leave your calendar blank for a few hours—or a few days—for unstructured recreation, to literally re-create yourself.

My mother, who lives in downtown Chicago, just spent a few days with us. At the age of eighty-one, she can be more clear about what happened forty years ago than about what happened this morning. So we talked about my sister and brother and me as toddlers and in elementary school and she told me, from the day I could walk, she could never catch up with me: "You were always running, running, running." I told her I had never stopped running, except for the few years when the boys were babies and my world slowed dramatically, shifting from airplanes and the bustle of the newsroom into the womb of my living room, years when I actually took sumptuous naps with the kids.

That was short-lived; again I am careening, this time from school to soccer to piano to karate. When I do nap, it's certainly not restful; napping means collapsing on a bed in twenty-minute spurts. I told my mother that life again too often feels like a flurry of autumn leaves in the wind. Time, our richest natural resource, is crunched and splintered and hurried. When I used to telephone friends,

I would ask, "Do you have two minutes?" These days I ask, "Do you have two seconds?" Lots of times the answer is no. My mother reminded me that the happiest time of her life was when she had three children to herself, seated around the dining room table in Oak Park.

"And it was over like this," she said, snapping her fingers. "So enjoy what you have and stop rushing around."

When the pace of life makes me start taking shallow gasps instead of deep, grounding breaths, I do force myself to halt in my tracks. New York psychotherapist Helene Brenner sees plenty of people with cyclone lives in the city she calls home. She views the mad dash as a way to keep their true selves at arm's length.

"Being super busy all the time can be a way to avoid facing what you have to face," Brenner says. "When you stop and really face yourself, that can hurt. So rather than allowing yourself to be depressed over some of the choices you have made in your life, you replace that with overbooking yourself. That way, there is no risk of leaving any psychological space to look at what you really need to look at. When you're always moving, you never have to be truly present with yourself."

I teach my journalism students at American University about maneuvering through the exploding information age. Yet as we talk about ways to flex the astounding tentacles of the Internet, I also stress that in their quest to acquire information, there is no substitution for a long conversation with someone, while you are staring into their eyes. That is the reason I encourage my mother to visit us often; I speak to her on the telephone every day, but it's not the same as having a glass of wine together at my kitchen table that is covered with a cloth that once draped her kitchen table.

It is only in extended face-to-face exchanges, rather than through voiceless communication, that intimacy can ferment, that truth can be uncovered. Good journalism, like solid relationships, unfolds over hours of sharing and digging. You get only superficial scrapings if you rely on phones and email. And in the quest to go face-to-face with yourself, you are also simply scratching the surface unless you give yourself the time and space to plow deeper. Give yourself the gift of time and make sure you take mini-vacations, be it for only an hour a day.

Surrendering to Yourself

Getting Naked with Yourself

I've talked a lot about excavation and unearthing in the process of getting to the self of truth. As I get older and bolder, one exercise I do in getting closer to that goal is to stand in front of a mirror, naked, and study that person, at every angle. Most people cringe at this suggestion, telling me they cannot bear to face the cellulite, love handles, mottled bellies from pregnancies, whatever it is about their bodies they consider ugly or imperfect. Of course, the criticism is illusory; lots of thin people think of themselves as huge.

But the mirror does not lie. And we need to quit lying in the quest to know ourselves. Facing yourself, dead-on, without clothes, in the flesh, is a giant step forward. It's cheating to take a thirty-second glance, you need to go in there and take a hard, ten-minute view. Don't forget to take a hand mirror and check out the rear. That creature is you, who you really are, and you may as well accept her, raw and naked, rather than deny her, hate her, wish she weighed in like Jennifer Aniston (who probably thinks she's fat).

Following a scrutinizing evaluation, you may decide to

go on a serious diet. You may decide to join a gym—the Jewish Kabbalists believe that only with a strong body can you have a strong soul. You may embrace your chubbiness. I love it when a large woman dresses well, shows off cleavage, and is proud of her bigness. Confidence is an intoxicating quality; no one dare call a big woman who loves herself "fat." Getting power from the mirror goes a long way. Getting naked with yourself means getting naked with your spirit.

Over the years the mirror has become my friend. I look into my own eyes and come up with answers to my deepest questions. I like the new muscles from weight lifting, the sharpened shoulders, the bands in my biceps, but I am no fool: this will never be the body of a twenty-one-year-old, nor would I want it to be. That was then, now is now, and this is probably as good as it's going to get after four pregnancies. When I look at myself, I'm not thinking what other people will think; I'm thinking of what I think of me.

Yet, sometimes I'm in the mirror dressing for a night out with Chuck, a Victoria Secret black sweater, low neck, old, soft jeans, high boots. And there's a fluttery expectation, as I think about how he'll think I look. I catch myself and say aloud: "How do *you* think you look?" And again, I see that although I hope my husband still finds me attractive, I picked these favorite clothes and I dressed for me, not for him.

Since I first became a student in the art of primping as an adolescent girl growing up with Twiggy as a prevailing goddess, gazing in the mirror has evoked intense emotions, many of those emotions centered around how I would appear to my man of the moment. Does he like my curly hair or should I Dippity Do it straight? Should I wear flat shoes to appear shorter? Should I wear pink lipstick or is he more of a red person? Will he think I'm too sloppy if I wear blue jeans?

I would bet that I'm not the lone woman who did, or still does, this questioning in the mirror, coming up with ways we can please our men with our appearances, and not asking ourselves what pleases us. Today, my relationship with the mirror is between me and myself, there is no imaginary guy judging the overall picture, giving his stamp of rejection or approval. My gut tells me when my naked body needs tuning or toning, whether jeans or a skirt are more fitting for an event, what lipstick shade to wear. When you are in the mirror primping not for a hot date but for yourself, you leave the house with a luminescent aura and killer energy.

After a shower, dry off in the mirror, don't look away, stand still for a while. Stay naked, walk around your bedroom, feel the cool air on your damp skin; feel everything you can't feel when you are constricted in clothing. Be aware of your body in concert with your soul, not as a separate piece of self.

Tell yourself, "Here I am, all of me," when you are splendidly naked. Worship the goddess within the sacred temple that houses the soul; celebrate the marriage of physical, cerebral, spiritual. Too often we treat the body as if it were separate from self; we dress it up, we dose it with medicines when it seems ailing, we put a jacket on it when it is cold, but the body seems alien to the self within. Being naked alone, and really being there, brings your entire organism into one consciousness. Mind and body becomes one seamless self, and your mind knows that a sacred temple should be treated royally, with healthy foods, sufficient rest, exercise, pampering.

I love soaking in a bath in the early morning, my hair floating, feeling every drop of hot water on every inch of me. I imagine I'm a nymph in a pond with lily pads, like the naked young women in John William Waterhouse's turn-of-the-century painting *Hylas and the Nymphs,* tresses wild, souls unmasked. Feeling comfortable with our nakedness frees us to penetrate our naked essence. It is only then that we can discern the most subtle waves of self.

Becoming Your Fantasy Self

Many people want to be exactly who they are. Most people yearn for a different life. Most people have abandoned childhood passions. Too many people feel like victims of circumstances, rather than masters of their destiny. Too many people surrender, without questioning.

I ask a wealthy woman in Houston whose only job is to be hostess for her husband's frequent business entertaining, "Are you living your dreams?" And she answers, "I'm not living my dreams in the sense that they're *my* dreams, but it's certainly a dreamlike life." There's a difference between leading a dreamy life and a life that stems from your own dreams. Most people have untapped potential; they have everything in front of them and they don't realize they have the power to unlock that vision. It's no easy task.

Our spiritual acuity is often muddied by the minutiae that fills our days, family logistics, career demands. Simply put, we forget to dream big. Sometimes I have nightmares of being on an airplane that falls and falls, but never hits the ground. I wake in a panic and immediately start making promises to myself to jump-start dreams and to hurl dead weight overboard. Those nightmares frighten me, but leave me more aware of the fragility of life. I rearrange things, scrambling out of lethargy and into action.

Senior year of college, a journalism professor assigned my class to profile someone whose job we wanted. I was twenty, and my dream was to become a correspondent who traveled the universe and reported on world events. As my profile subject, I chose Mel Wax, then the anchor of *Newsroom* on KQED, San Francisco's public television station. I spent a day with Wax, the former mayor of Sausalito, trailing him like an enamored puppy, around the city and through the preparation and delivery of the evening broadcast. After that February day in 1976, I was irrevocably bitten by the news business, it was where I belonged. I loved its impact, its reach, the reporter's way—Mel Wax was unflappable, cool, wry.

Yet after twenty-five years as a journalist, I still ask myself at times: Who would you be if you weren't who you are? I will never give up writing, for it is an appendage, permanent, like a leg or an arm. At midlife, however, there are stirrings beyond journalism I must pay attention to, tempting fantasies that dare me to make them real. One of them is to become more involved in medicine, a field I've been fascinated by since I was a child.

My grandfather Henry Krasnow was among the first Russian doctors to settle in Chicago, and biology was one of my favorite subjects in high school. When I was seven, my parents bought me a book called *The Human Body*. Flipping through the clear plastic pages, a large naked man turned into a skeleton, and I memorized the maze of muscles and the composition of organs and bones, and how the intricate body systems worked. As a second grader, I remember sitting on the stairs in our house, my mother helping me buckle my red rubber boots, and reciting the path of digestion, from the enzymes in saliva breaking down food to the exit of waste through the large intestine. I delighted in knowing how sound is heard and in being able to spell *auditory ossicles*, the tiny, vibrating bones in the ear.

Years later, when I was studying for my master's in liberal studies at Georgetown University, my focus of study was in science and public policy, with courses centered on brave new worlds in cell biology and gene therapy. My thesis traced the moral and ethical ramifications of advanced fertility techniques. Of all the famous people and edgy social trends I have covered as a journalist, unraveling the role of science in baby-making, from in vitro fertilization to human cloning, was my most stimulating, often shocking, assignment yet.

In profile writing, you get to the bottom of someone's personality; in science, you get to the bottom of life itself, and

I loved the depths I was able to travel to. While talking to ethicists and theologians about the new reproductive technologies, I was astounded by how the baby business could explode into an ethical and legal nightmare, revolving around questions such as "Who owns this fetus, anyway?" From grandmothers gestating with their infertile daughter's eggs and birthing their own granddaughters to sperm donors suing for visitation rights, believe-it-or-not births make straight IVF seem about as routine as a face-lift. I remain captivated by the quagmires that lie ahead for the tens of thousands of children whose lives began in laboratories.

I am too old to start medical school, but am still young in my discovery of science and medicine, and I remain childlike in my excitement for *The New England Journal of Medicine* and the *Mayo Clinic Family Health Book,* which I page through all the time. I have no idea where this layperson's obsession with medical research will lead, but the question mark is enticing. And I'm thrilled to be learning new things at my age, just for learning's sake.

As I discover other facets of myself, I am driven to move beyond the tight web of family into the community. I grew up Jewish in a predominantly non-Jewish suburb, and a wise and wild Sunday-school teacher named Al Jablon helped show me as an adolescent that I could have a religious identity that was different from that of most of my friends and still be cool. We are raising our children in a predominantly non-Jewish area of Maryland, and I want to give back what I got to early teens, who are at an age when developing and accepting one's self apart from the pack is paramount. And so I have recently begun teaching an eighth-grade religious-school class at our temple. It feels great to keep stretching beyond who I was yesterday.

I urge you to listen to what's beckoning you, to keep acquiring knowledge, to take dives into the unknown. There is no time to stall. As a citizen of an unstable world you certainly understand the necessity of living urgently now, of taking risks. Be assertive in chasing your dreams and your goals. Don't scatter your shots: Listen to your gut yearnings, and target the top five things you'd like to accomplish in the next two years. Prioritize them, then start shaking things up. Dreams can seem so distant and ethereal that they will never be yours to grasp. Yet you can never know what is possible unless you first make the leap.

I'm in a gift shop in the Grand Canyon looking at a poster of a mountain goat in midair, leaping from one peak to another, a one-mile drop separating the cliffs. "He made it," reads the caption below the photograph. When considering daring feats we don't know if we are going to make it, but we will never know unless we make the jump. The greatest barriers to success and growth exist only in your imagination. Forging onward takes clearing your mind of negative energy.

Last spring, as the buds turned into tulips and irises and lilies in my garden, there was still a black fog marring my consciousness, separating me from experiencing the bloom of the moment. This sadness I could not shake was from the endless news broadcasts I was taking in daily to keep up with Israel, Iraq, Afghanistan, and the obscene number of child kidnappings in America. I care deeply about what is happening in the world, but the twisted images of death, grieving parents, and wars were blocking me from being in my life; I was swept instead into universal distress.

One recent afternoon I was in the backyard with my sons Jack and Zane, who were meticulously arranging dozens of sticks into tepees and miniature log cabins. I was staring right at them as they ran into the woods, retrieved sticks, whittled off ragged edges with their Swiss army knives, and knelt on the ground to build. Yet as they raced through the grass and whooped about their creations, I was not there although I was there. Even when they squealed, "Mom, look at this!" I would look but wouldn't see, because I was stuck in a world of global anguish, not the world in front of me, of kids and their stick structures.

At that moment, in the backyard with twin eight-year-olds who were clamoring for my attention while I was looking right through them with a frozen smile, I made a decision to stop watching the news five times a day, that it was messing up my mind and zapping my ability to be where I am. I watch one news recap a night now, after the boys are asleep. It is impossible to do my work, as a mother and as an author who wants to convey hopeful messages, with a perpetually twisted gut.

We can control the stimuli we take in. We can choose to be bombarded by rousing, positive life forces, and not be downed by grisly hallucinations. When I awaken, I stand on our hill with my arms outstretched in thanksgiving, and embrace the sky and the morning and the warmth of the rising sun. It's just me and the universe, and I say to God and myself and whatever other spirits may be listening: "I am grateful for being alive. Please give me the strength to be my best, most compassionate self today." Set your alarm clock a half hour earlier and create your own affirming ritual outdoors. When it's just you and the sun and the sky and the dawn, you can get to your soul a whole lot faster. I feel like Albert Camus, who wrote in his *Notebooks 1935–1942:* "Today is a resting place, and my heart goes out to meet itself. . . . I do not know what I could wish for rather than this continued presence of self with self. What I want now is not happiness but awareness."

There are other things I do to rid my psyche of the dark clouds that obscure present-mindedness. I rarely listen to news radio in my car; I made a CD of all my favorite love ballads of the last thirty years, from Al Green's "I'm Still in Love with You" to John Lennon's "Woman," and that's what I soak in as I beat around town. The music is rich and reverberating, even the sad songs, and my being becomes lighter. We can be who we want to be if we don't lose consciousness, if we don't take on the woes of the planet, but concentrate on fortifying our own attitudes, and fully loving the people who occupy our own little worlds.

We must be supremely grateful for the bounty that is ours, thanking God for what we have, again and again. The more gratitude we express to our spiritual masters, the more space opens up within us to love more, do more, and be a force for change in the universe. It doesn't have to be as president of a country. You can transform the world by working on one person at a time.

On vacation in Arizona, the boys are spending the

afternoon go-karting with Chuck and Uncle Greg, my brother, and I make an appointment at a salon for a pedicure. I am assigned to CeCe, a wisp of a woman with the face of an angel. As she is massaging oil up and down my calves, I tell her I'm an author and mention the title of this book. Brown eyes flashing, she looks up at me with a beatific smile and says, "I am surrendering to myself— finally." This woman from South America who sloughs off dead skin from calloused, dirty feet for a living is a person with a regal manner and glow.

Having feet in your face all day may not be your fantasy job, but CeCe absolutely loves what she does, because she considers it a way of "serving other people and giving them happiness." She was steamrolled by life for many years, living in poverty and with abusive men, but she always persevered, and today she tells her twenty-year-old daughter: "Don't let any man put you down. Don't let any boss put you down. Be proud of yourself." CeCe is proud of herself, as you will see:

It gives me a good feeling to know that I can make people happy. You know, sometimes people need a little touching; they don't have anybody to touch them. I especially love to take care of the feet of the elderly; as you get older, you can't cut your toenails and they really need me to take care of their feet. Actually the bottom of your foot has the nerve endings of all the organs in the body. You can find the kidney and the heart and the liver and the gallbladder. I believe I help heal people.

People ask me: "How can you work with dirty feet all

day?" I don't think that way. How many jobs are there where you are doing something that people appreciate right away? You can really see it in their faces. They say thank you, thank you, over and over again. That's my reward. I am appreciated every day.

All my life I've been helping others. Still, I have made a lot of foolish mistakes in my life. I was born in Colombia. I come from a large family—five sisters, a brother—a very, very poor family. My mother worked many jobs, and because my father always got himself in trouble with the law, he would be in and out of jail. We all lived in a small house with one bathroom.

My mother would leave us for many hours by ourselves because she had to go out and find jobs to make ends meet. Sometimes our mother would be gone so long we didn't know where she was. And so we pretty much had to find everything for ourselves. My mother got up very early and she would usually leave a big pot of soup for the day. And if there was no pot of soup, we would go all day with nothing to eat until she got home.

I had three other sisters who had left for the United States. My father ended up in jail again and my mother reported him missing and it was in the Colombia newspapers, and one of my sisters in Miami used to buy those papers and she saw the report about our father. So she decided to fly to Colombia to see what was going on, and she asked me to come back and live with her in Florida. I was twelve and she became my legal guardian.

After my third year in high school I felt like I could not stay with my sister anymore. She was very aggressive; she would say

to me "Just remember you are in this country because of me."
My sister treated me like a maid. I had to cut the grass, do the
laundry, take her child out to the park. I was not allowed to
have friends over. I used to tell her: "The minute I turn
eighteen, I'm going to be leaving this house because this is not
the way I want to live." I had a sister in California, and I called
her and asked her if I could come live with her. And so I moved
again, and I had my last year of high school in California.

I met this guy two months before prom and he asked me to
marry him, and I decided that would be the best thing for me
to do. I married him in June after graduation, and the marriage lasted two months. Again I moved, this time to San Francisco, and I worked in the University of San Francisco in the
library and took some college classes. While I was there I met
this man who was in the military at the Presidio. And I happened to fall in love. He was from Colombia too, we had a lot
in common. I was twenty-one years old. He was twenty-seven.

He got moved with the military from San Francisco to
Georgia, and then I could no longer keep my mind on my
books. I had to be with him, I was loving him so much. And I
decided that the best thing was to move back to Florida so I
could be closer to him. So I packed all my bags and left again,
and on my way to Florida I stopped in Georgia and I got pregnant that weekend. And then when I told him, he was a
totally different person. He didn't want any responsibility
whatsoever; he didn't want to have any ties to me or his baby.
I decided to have the child because I don't believe in abor-
tions. So this is my son. He is twenty-four years. He has never
seen his father, his father has never seen him.

I got married again a few years ago, and my new husband's daughter lives in New Jersey. We visited there and I got a good idea, something I had to do—to stop by the father of my son's house. I had found out that he had left the military and was back in New Jersey, living with his mother. I don't know how this happened, it was spiritual magic, but for some reason I remembered the street name, but I could not remember the house number. Then we get to the street, the number came back to me. And I got out of the car and I knocked on the door. An old lady come to the door and said, "Can I help you?" I said, "Yes, is Juan home?" She said, "Well, let me go and see." Suddenly a man comes to the door and stares at me and it was him. After twenty-four years, I see him again.

And I say bravely, "Hello, Juan, I'm CeCe." And he just looks shocked, and then I say, "And this is my husband." And the two men shake hands and Juan says, "Come in." I tell him right away: "We are not looking for anything here." I don't want his money; I want him to feel like he has a son. We stay for only about a half hour, but I feel proud of myself. I had to do it, to close a chapter in my life, to put it all behind me.

My daughter, she comes from another very short second marriage. I was not in love with this guy whatsoever. I just felt like my son needed a father, a male role model in his life. We went to live in Chicago with his family because we didn't have much money, no furniture. And we both start to work at the Motorola factory, and we work hard and we get enough money to rent a little apartment. Shortly, I see things I am not happy about. He didn't come home after work and help with the chores. So after I work all day I come home, get my son from his grandparents' house, and do everything around the house. I was exhausted all the time.

One day I'm feeling so sad I call my mom, and even though she lives in the United States for thirty years, she never learned to speak English. So I talk to her on the phone in Spanish, and my husband gets so upset that he can't understand what I say and he thinks I'm talking about him. So when I finished talking on the phone, he got up and he hit me in the eye and broke my eyebrow bone. I was taken to the hospital and he was taken to jail for abusing me. I told the truth about the beating. I pack my stuff again and quickly move back to California.

But when I got to California, my husband followed me. He went to live with his brother, who was also in California, and I got pregnant. Our marriage did not last long after our daughter was born. So I married one person when I was very young, I followed a man I loved who didn't love me back. And I married another man who hit me. But I was getting smarter about the world. I begin to see it's a hard world for women. It started for me watching my mother keep getting my father out of jail and taking care of us by herself. Then I follow in my mother's footsteps; my son was three years old when my daughter was born, and it's just me and my children, no man.

The month after my daughter was born I had to go back to work, on a factory line at a company that made semiconductors. I was earning six dollars an hour working from three P.M. to eleven P.M.; then in the mornings and on the weekend I was cleaning houses. My mother had moved from Florida to

California, and she would stay home with my kids. I had a lot of pain going on inside of me, but I didn't really stop and think too much about my feelings. I had to keep going to make a living to feed my children.

You know, even though I was cleaning houses, I always told my kids whatever anyone does, respect them. Like the men who take out our garbage, I say that's a noble job. Somebody has to do that job. But sometimes I felt bad about myself and my struggles in life. I always just did what I had to do to get by. I had no parental guidance in terms of someone showing me "this is what you need to do to grow up and be successful." I learn everything myself. I never ask anybody for a penny.

Because of this, I am today a very strong person, and I teach my children to be strong, to hold their heads up. I tell them: "You have to take care of yourself. Don't let anybody run your life. Don't ever let anyone push you down in any way."

Because people did push me down, I thought for a long time that men were not good. I had no idea what a good marriage could be. I never saw my parents kissing, I never heard my father say "You look pretty today" to his wife, or give her flowers. So in many ways, I have trouble to become my own person, a happy person. But I actually broke the chain and got loose. I left all the situations where I was being treated like dirt. Like a dog.

I felt like I was a prisoner when I was living with my sister and with my second husband, and I tell you, I will never feel that way again. My husband now is Donald, and he's a very supportive man. But I was strong even before I met him. My daughter knows to be strong, too: I tell her all the time:

"Don't put up with garbage from a man, from anyone. Get you life in order so you know what you want. I don't want you to depend on anyone. You have to depend on yourself. We don't need to depend on a man to be happy and survive."

I have taught my daughter so much about being her own self. She knows how to check the oil in her car, how to change spark plugs and tires. I just got to a point in my life where I realized I don't have to put up with anything anymore. For a long time I worked for the postal service, and I went through a lot of garbage there: You don't know stress until you work in a post office. Finally, when my kids got into their twenties I said to myself, "Now my kids can earn their own livings." I got my license in cosmetology. And that was the big change in my life.

We left California, moved to Arizona, and now I live in a beautiful place, in the mountains. I have sadness in my heart sometimes, but I give people so much happiness with pedicures and manicures and facials, my heart gets happy again.

My life could be something many people can learn from: do what you feel is good for you, and don't put up with men or jobs that bring you down. Look for happiness inside of you; nobody is going to come and give it to you. I'm forty-five now, and I do wish there would come a day that I could finish college. But I've done good in this life. You know, my kids have never gone to bed without food. And I have found peace within myself. I know what I really want out of my life, and that is to fill up the cup of my soul every day. And with the work I do, I really get to fill up the cup. I love giving pedicures, to see somebody's face when they are relaxed. I love when I hear them say, "That feels so good."

LIFE, DEATH, AND THE GRAND CANYON

Sitting with CeCe for an hour in a Tucson salon was the heavenly break I needed after a tour northward through the state that had plenty of hellish moments. While most tourists who visit the Grand Canyon are awed by the majesty of nature and life, on our trip there along the South Rim I am obsessed with death. Staring one mile down into the abyss, I am struck by how easy it would be to go splat. It's this filament of a line between life and death that sends me into wracking tears on our first stop off the tour bus, at an overlook into a jagged cavern that reminds me of a giant shark's mouth, wide open, ready to swallow us. At the second that I'm losing it, Chuck props our four sons against an ill-constructed guardrail made of three pieces of pipe with sixteen-inch spaces between them, set at the outer rim of sheer rock face. He is posing them for a picture, and makes them stand there for a while. And I'm watching, horrified, imagining a stumble, caused by imbalance or a blast of wind, and one of the children falling through the gaping railing.

It is nine A.M., Easter morning. The park is vacant and I am sitting cross-legged on a pine-needle-covered patch of ground twenty yards from the family, my head buried in my hands. My oldest son, Theo, walks over to me, taps me on the shoulder, and says, "Come on, Mom, push through your fears. You gotta see this." I walk with Theo to the ledge, and clutching the rail, I push myself to gaze straight down the cliff, even though my knees are shaking and it feels like someone has blasted helium into my chest. Slowly I am soothed by the landscape, luminous and endless, and Theo's tight grip around my shoulders. Standing one mile high, I look up at the clouds, and instead of fearing that I'm about to drop into a black hole, I have a vision of myself floating upward to God, to perpetual light.

Then I flip back into a downward mode, with this macabre thought: "I wonder what it would feel like to hurl myself in." Yet it's not so much a suicide wish as a burst of invincibility, a desire to become at one with the burnt-red rocks, spiraling into the Colorado River, which snakes mysteriously through the mesa and into the unknown. As a piece of the Grand Canyon, I would have an eternal, vast life.

The children and Chuck have hiked ahead on the trail, and I stand alone at the rail, shaking less, stomach settling, calming myself with rhythmic breaths. I am thinking now of my preteen son—a boy who will go on any roller coaster or climb on a rope course to the top of a five-story tree and zip-line down—advising his mother to conquer her fright. My lifelong fear of heights, of course, is really a fear of death. And I know, we all know, if we could just surmount our fear of dying we would truly be invincible. On his own journey of transformation from Harvard professor to Baba Ram Dass to simply Ram Dass, Dr. Richard Alpert, the *Be Here Now* guru, says that along his cosmic and convoluted path, he has somehow left his own fear of death behind:

"The fear of death seems somehow to have flown the coop somewhere along the way in this game," writes Ram Dass in *The Only Dance There Is*. "It certainly changes the nature of my living experience every day because each day can be whatever it is, and it's all right. I'm not collecting something to avoid something later."

My mother is without fear of death because she has already been through the worst experiences anyone could live through. During her teens, having fled her hometown of Warsaw for Paris, she received word that her mother and sister and brother and five nieces and one nephew had been slaughtered in Hitler's death camps. Her father had died earlier of a heart attack. When my father died, her husband of thirty-four years, she was overwhelmed with sadness, but she did not fall apart. To Helene Krasnow, life is life, death is death, and that's that.

At our kitchen table recently I recorded my octogenarian mom on tape, and here is how she views her own death, which, if she keeps up with her workouts with a personal trainer and remains disease-free, could still be years away. She speaks in a thick Eastern European accent and I've cleaned up her vocabulary:

I lost my parents, my sister, my brothers, everybody. When I lost your father, I had been alone before, so I knew how to survive, I went on. I was strong, I thought, "If Hitler didn't get me, nothing will."

But I depended on your father very much. I didn't work, I was raising you. To me, you were my life. You kids were my centerpiece. And when he is gone, I still have you, which is reason to go on living. I was only sixty-five years old when your father died; he was sixty-seven, and that's too young to die. Your sister thought I should go talk to someone, so she arranged for me to see a psychologist at Northwestern University. And the shrink interviewed me and I told her everything and she said to me: "Mrs. Krasnow, you are okay. You are going to be okay. You don't need this."

I was strong when I met him, but I think your father made me stronger. He taught me so many things. He was always so busy with work and so busy with meetings, I learned to do everything myself. Before I met your father, I didn't even know how to write a check. He said to me, "Sit down, you need to learn this because you're going to do all the house bills." And I took over all the bills right away. And I thank him because when he died, I knew how to take care of things.

Maybe I was in love too much with your father, because when he died, I'm not interested in other men. I didn't need a man. I have you kids and I have eight grandchildren, and they give me the will to stay alive as long as I can. Most widows I know look to get married right away. But they are just different people. They don't have the confidence in themselves, or maybe they don't want to be alone. I've been alone before, and I can be alone. It's better than being with another husband you don't like as much as the first husband.

No, I didn't fall apart when your father died, I didn't fall apart when I lost my family. Since I was a teenager, I've been used to doing things for myself, and I've always been able to keep moving. I'll tell you when I fell apart for a few days— when you kids made me quit cigarettes after smoking for fifty years. But I've never felt lost. I left Poland and I went to France and I didn't speak French and I learned French. I left France and moved to America and didn't speak English and I learned English. I found my way wherever I was.

I am sad to be without your father, but this is my life now, you children. To me, to see your happiness and my grandchildren, smart, such grandchildren, who else has? It's so hard to believe. After all the death I have seen, I have so much life around me.

I could live another five or ten years, I don't know, but I'm not afraid of dying. I will go to sleep, and that's it. I won't see anything. I won't feel anything. Every night you go to sleep, and you're dead for eight hours. When it's the real death, it's the same thing. I hope I pass away at night. The life I lived, I could have been dead any time. I could have been in a concentration camp, but I was not. I lived through hell. I ate out of garbage cans so I wouldn't starve during the war. I lost everybody. So nothing scares me. I'm not scared to go on planes. When it's my time, goodbye, I have loved this life.

I don't believe there is a next life. This is my life and this is it. But I talk to your father, and I believe he is still guiding me, like he did at the beginning of our marriage. I am right now a healthy woman, except for a pain in my back from arthritis. And you can't be my age without thinking of dying once in a while. But most of the time I think about today. I cry a little bit, but not too much. What for? People have it much worse than this. I am not a lonely woman being alone. I know myself very well—oh boy, do I know myself. I know what I'm made of. So I go through some turbulence in my life, I still have myself, yes?

Well, I'm not the same person as when I was young and

pretty in France. Now I see lots of wrinkles in the mirror. But I don't see myself like an old person, because so much of my mind is still here. I've got the energy still, and energy keeps you alive. I still have too much happiness coming to die. I am still here, yes, and you three children and your children is what I've created. I lost one family and I have a big family here. What's to cry about?

Her stoicism eases me in an unsettled world and helps me snap out of overly anxious moods, which she reacts to dismissively with: "It's nothing compared to the world I saw." I am also inspired by the inhabitants of Israel, who continue to ride buses and eat at cafés despite weekly suicide bombings and having to live amid charred carcasses of buildings. After eating breakfast together, parents and their school-age children go their own ways, uncertain whether they will see each other at day's end. I want what they have, courage at the core.

I need what they have right now.

At this writing, all police forces in the Washington area are still searching for the sniper who has shot thirteen people in Maryland and Virginia during the past twenty-one days. Ten of the victims died, good people picked off at random filling their tanks at gas stations, coming out of stores, one was mowing his lawn. A thirteen-year-old boy was entering middle school at eight A.M. when he was hit in the chest, twenty-five minutes from our house. Our schools have been on lockdown, which means there are no sports events, no recess, the fall festivals we await all year are canceled. We are in siege mentality, moving quickly from buildings to our cars, terrorized, terrified.

Shootings and wars make me more fervent in my workouts, sweating out the fear, determined to become as strong as I can be, to rid myself of grisly thoughts. It's the only way to cope with this madness. And months after these killers were caught, there is still much madness. Muscles, I am convinced, give us more far-reaching souls and strengthen our resolve to carry on with optimism. When the late Senator Paul Wellstone, a former wrestling champion with fierce convictions, was diagnosed with multiple sclerosis, he shrugged off questions about how this would affect his performance with this response: "I have a strong body. I have a strong heart. I have a strong soul." Indeed, many Americans will remember Wellstone as the soul of the Senate, one of the lone voices to speak out against the invasion of Iraq.

We all need strong souls, sun in our hearts, when darkness is everywhere; a heart weakened by despair cannot hold out very long. We need to be brave.

"People living deeply have no fear of death," writes Anaïs Nin. What am I doing wrong? I live deeply, but I have an unrelenting fear of death these days, more for my children than for myself. Perhaps, I need to go deeper— deeper into faith, deeper into my soul. I am trying, and it is hard, so hard; evil murderers have come too close. I see evil's eyes, the irises are yellow slits; I feel evil's hot breath, steamy and foul. Perhaps our fundamental fear of death comes from humankind's need to control, and a mistrust of the unknown. In John White's book *A Practical Guide to*

Death & Dying, the author quotes this passage from Socrates, just before he drank the hemlock: "To fear death, gentlemen, is nothing other than to think oneself wise when one is not; for it is to think one knows what one does not know. No man knows whether death may not even turn out to be the greatest of blessings for a human being, and yet people fear it as if they knew for certain that it is the greatest of evils."

Are you ready for death? What brings me closer to fearlessness is focusing not on dying but on making certain the life I lead is raw and right and real. To lose that ultimate fear is to live an unbridled life. Because it could happen to any of us, any of our siblings, any of our parents, at any time.

John Turney was forty-three when he was diagnosed with stage four colon cancer Labor Day weekend 1997. The oldest of four children, the only son, and father of his own two young sons, John was six-foot-four, a champion at sailing, tennis, and golf. He had never been seriously ill a day in his life, there was no history of cancer in his family. His sister, Barb Heussler, was "in total shock" the day her parents called to tell her that John, a rising star in commercial real estate in Chicago, had a disease that could kill him, and did in January 1999, after a valiant fight. Here is how Barb describes before and after "the unthinkable happened":

John was the epitome of a healthy, vital young man. He was very successful in his real estate firm, traveling to Japan all the time, where he had a large account. And he was on his way to being even more successful; he was definitely on the A-track, ascending quickly. You should have seen him, lean and tall, the All-American boy, married happily for seventeen years. At the time he was diagnosed, his boys were nine and twelve.

I always felt like we had the perfect family growing up: four kids, very close, parents who stayed married, both of them are still alive. So to have something like this happen was particularly shocking; you read about these things, but these things happen to someone else, these things do not happen to you. At first John's attitude, everyone's attitude, was: "We are going to beat this. We are not going to give in." Everyone in my family is very competitive in sailing and tennis, and we have this inherent fighting attitude; you don't just roll over, you win.

But when his cancer was found, it was so advanced, it was an impossible fight to win. We clung to the hope that miracles happen and doctors sometimes do save hopeless cases, but it was not to be with John. His own spirit was amazing; after his first surgery when they got the cancer out of the colon and found it had spread to his liver and lungs, he still carried on fairly normally. There was a big sailing regatta in Bermuda that his son was sailing in, and he was determined to go and watch him, and he did. His biggest struggle was participating in the Mackinac Race, crewing on a 46-foot sailboat for 330 miles and thirty-six hours, from Chicago to the tip of Lake Michigan. He was weak and undergoing chemo and the voyage was very strenuous, but he just had to do it, and he did.

When we were children, we three girls always knew John would take care of us. He was the big, strong, older brother, and we could count on him for anything. He looked after us almost like a parent does. Three years after his death, it is a loss that still won't go away. I know it will never go away. My family gathers often at our parents' home in Florida, and even though there are now nine grandchildren, there is a heavy sadness that our whole family will never again be intact.

I will never again think that tragedy is something that brushes other people and not me; once you have this experience, you realize the frailty of life and that anything can happen to anybody, no matter who you are or how lucky you have been. I hug my children more than ever after losing my brother. I hug them so hard they push me away, and I don't care. My parents have been through hell. Your kids in their forties are not supposed to die before you. It's devastating. It's wrong. For all of us, I doubt we will ever be able to experience full-throttle happiness again. Something is missing, and we will never get it back.

I'm not a religious person, but I feel John's spirit every day. I believe that he's here with us because you are all part of each other when you're a family. We have his essence. He wrote his own eulogy in the form of a letter to his family and friends, and this line no one at the funeral will ever forget: "Remember, the wind contains all the words that have ever been spoken. My words are in there also. So listen to God's breath."

The other day, my husband and I were on our sailboat with our two sons, and on the CD player was the 10,000 Maniacs singing "These Are Days." We were out on a perfect day, spectacular wind, heeling over, and I'm holding my nine-year-old Bennett, and twelve-year-old Brendan is hanging on the back of the boat. My husband and I got tears in our eyes, listening to the words: "These are days you'll remember.

Never before and never since, I promise, will the whole world be warm as this."

These are the days, and I took a photo of that moment in my mind, of the four of us. Because you never know what can happen. But at that moment, everything was perfect.

The first time I really focused on death was in the sixth grade when I read *Death Be Not Proud*, a memoir by John Gunther describing his only child, Johnny, who died at the age of seventeen after battling aggressive brain cancer for fifteen months. I remember being stunned that someone so young could die, that I could die. Johnny, with his "hair the color of wheat out in the sun," was a remarkable child, shrewd and precocious, telling his dad by the age of six that he knew already who God was: "God is what's good in me."

I kept reading and rereading the paragraph in which Gunther describes Johnny's last breath before he died at 11:02 P.M., June 30, 1947:

> *I felt his arms, cupping my hands around them, and the warmth gradually left them, receding very slowly upward from his hands. For a long time some warmth remained. Then little by little, the life-color left his face, his lips became blue, and his hands were cold.*
>
> *What is life? It departs covertly. Death took him.*

Death took him. I read this as a healthy eleven-year-old, imagining gigantic arms extending from the sky and snatching this child from his mother and his father and his misery. Then people started dying who were part of my life: my parents' friends, my friends' parents, a neighbor, my grandmother, two college friends in a car accident, my father. And I developed a fascination with death, not a sick one, but a journalist's curiosity to understand the facts of death, which I've come to know is impossible.

In the late 1980s, when I was a feature writer for United Press International, I spent a day interviewing Elisabeth Kübler-Ross on her 250-acre farm, Healing Waters, in the Shenandoah hills of Virginia. Kübler-Ross, the author of the landmark book *On Death and Dying*, was an unquestioning believer in afterlife. I was drawn to Kübler-Ross because my father had just died, and I was knotted by grief, hopeful about reincarnation. At the time of our interview, the Swiss-born author and doctor wanted to start a hospice for AIDS babies on her land. Some residents in her ultraconservative county were so appalled that she had received several threats that her farm would be burned down. Years later Healing Waters did burn down and arson was suspected.

I asked her if she ever feared for her life.

"No, I feel totally protected," said Kübler-Ross, laughing softly. "And if I have to make the transition, I'm certainly not afraid of it."

She picked up an orange velour caterpillar from a basket on the floor. "This is what I show to dying children. I tell them, 'Your body is just a caterpillar. When you die, the caterpillar will release the butterfly.'" Kübler-Ross reached into a slit in the caterpillar and pulled out a tiny monarch butterfly.

"And I tell them, 'The butterfly is the immortal part of the human being that flies up. The only thing that is mortal, the body, goes back to the soil.'"

When I recounted this story in *Surrendering to Motherhood*, I was uplifted by Kübler-Ross, who made me believe that even though my father's body was lowered into the icy ground of Chicago, his spirit was freed, alive in me, my sister, my brother, my mother, all the people who loved him; a spirit that somehow could still soar in our lives.

Reflecting on spirits released postmortem as I write *Surrendering to Yourself*, I am certain that our spirit must be freed while we are alive, that the butterfly of the soul must fly before we die. Many Christian friends tell me the best is yet to come, that heaven is *it*, but I cannot live that way. What is now, this minute, is my heaven on earth, my moment to do my best and give my all and act on the passions of the soul. And if there is an afterlife, I'll give it my best shot there, too.

Paul McCartney visited George Harrison's bedside as Harrison lay dying from advanced cancer in December 2001. McCartney was quoted as saying "that George Harrison was laughing in the face of madness." Holding Harrison's hand, McCartney said his friend who loved sitars and fast cars was not afraid to move on; he knew that all things must pass, the title of his 1970 album. The multifaceted and indefatigable Harrison—early devotee of the Maharishi Mahesh Yogi, owner of a purple McLaren sports car, survivor of multiple stab wounds by a deranged fan—left behind a legacy that will never pass. He was fifty-eight, an old soul who could laugh at mortality, entering the next phase with joy in his heart rather than bitterness, an exemplary way to leave this stage.

There are many close family members I count on for well-being; my husband, mother, sister, brother, my father's sister Aunt Gloria. Lately, I've been thinking the unthinkable, the grim reality of losing these people, unfailing relationships that hold the collective memory of my life. These are the folks who define who I am.

Knowing that my circle of family, here, now, is ephemeral makes me work harder at developing permanence from within, something George Harrison had; an ability to stand solidly while gusts and gales buffeted him. I know death awaits someone I love, lurking around the corner, I need to be ready, but how can one be ready? By loving with a vengeance. Now.

My husband's mother died nine months ago. His father died in 1994. The first morning Chuck woke up with no parents, I lay next to him, my head under his chin, lightly stroking his back. Our children were laughing at the inane blare of the Cartoon Network on the television in the next room. Theo's voice was the loudest, booming with the huskiness of adolescence. I thought of how pure and immense is our love for our children. And I told Chuck that I knew no one could ever love a son like a mother does, but that I loved him a whole lot, more than he knew.

He hugged the breath out of me, and said that hearing he was fully loved at the moment he was feeling the hollowness of a new orphan meant everything. It's easy to tell your spouse "I love you," and it goes a long way. It's also easy to forget to exchange even a few cordial sentences with husbands and wives in the course of an overscheduled day. Don't forget to tell the people you love "I love you." All we have is this one moment, this one chance. A good friend just lost her forty-eight-year-old husband to a heart attack. This could be me, this could be you.

I grasp tightly to this moment each time I am with my aging mother, who I have come to appreciate now more than ever. When I was a child, she was stern more than cuddly, her hugs quick and hard. In the late afternoon we would sometimes find her on the smoky-blue chair in the living room, crying over the loss of her family. We tiptoed around her. No laughter or fooling around could ever completely dissipate her long-held sadness, a cloud that never entirely left our house. But I could count on my mother. She routinely prepared lunches that were waiting on the table at noon—local elementary schools in the 1960s did not have cafeterias— and without fail, she would be waiting at the door at 3:10 P.M. to greet her three children who had walked home from their school a block away. Most days she could be found sitting at the kitchen table, knitting us sweaters and doing crossword puzzles, wearing black stretch pants, a flowered apron, and a striped kitchen towel draped over her shoulder.

As I raise my own children and make my own mistakes, I see that my mother may not have been classically maternal, but she did the best job she could do, considering she herself was mother-less at an early age. She was impeccably organized and gave us structure and predictability, and those are gifts that go a long way.

I have grown to love my mother in ways I never loved her, as I've been able to share with her how my childhood felt, hear her side of the story, and come to discover her wild, funny side. Now that we've reached this level of honesty, she's got only a few more years left and I already feel the ache of loss that lies ahead. So we have her visit us often, and she teaches our children things they would never learn anywhere else. And when old, bad blood between us starts to surface, I try to hold my tongue and just love her. I realize that she is needy of my love in her eighties in the same way I was needy of her love when I was a child. Yet, because I never knew the pain that she knows, I am able to give love without restraint; that is my gift back to her.

I encourage all of you to get to a place with your own aging parents where you are not angry but open, and let sadness pass, even rage. Let it go. Probe your mothers and fathers about things you've always wanted to know. The last thing any of us wants are unanswered questions after it's too late. We can never know ourselves if we don't allow ourselves to know our parents, and that takes getting close to them, and that can be tough. Because getting close to our parents means we will see pieces of ourselves we've been trying to avoid. Yet there are too many middle-aged children who wish they had made the effort and forgiven while they still had mothers and fathers around.

We spend much of our lives trying to be nothing like our parents, only to emerge as adults to find that we're actually very much like them. As I drive home from the Baltimore airport after dropping off my mom, I am reminded that the same stuff bugs me about her that has always bugged me about her—sponging off counters the split second a spill occurs, haranguing me that my skirts are too short and my hair is too long, telling everybody what to do, moving through the house like a tornado.

As I complained to my husband that night, he got a strange expression on his face and said, "The apple doesn't fall too far from the tree. You're just like her." All I knew in the 1970s at the peak of the women's movement was that I didn't want to grow up to be like my mother, dish towel slung over my shoulder, knitting. Yet I have grown up to be like my mother. I knit and I'm manic about order and I usually have a wet dish towel slung over a shoulder, one I use immediately whenever anyone spills at a meal, which is all the time.

Over the years I would sometimes feel that I hated my mother, and told her so. Yet even after the nastiest of exchanges, we always kissed and made up and persevered. And the reason I did this was not because I wasn't angry enough to cut off ties. It was because I was afraid she would die before I got to say I'm sorry, that I don't hate her, that I really love her. She is, after all, my mother. Unless parents are downright abusive, I believe we need to love them even if we despise them. We can't be free to become our true selves unless we let go of gnawing, venomous hatred for parents. We do not have to adore them, but we do need to forgive them. Holding on to hostility is a central block to our evolution.

One friend and I were talking about our parents and she

said she despises her father; they have had no contact for five years, and she instructed him in writing that if he ever has anything he wants to say to her, she will accept his words only in letter form. He may not telephone her, or show up at her house. I asked her how she would feel if he died, and she responded, "I feel like he died long ago." I don't know why this daughter and father have nothing to do with each other, and I didn't ask. What I do know is that I am happy my mother is still alive, and relieved that we have pushed through a lot of hard history into a new relationship

She is too old for me to dump old pain on her. It's my problem, not hers, and I can deal with it, I must deal with it, in order to be the best mother of my own children. It is tiresome to listen to midlifers blame their dysfunctional families for their inability to grow up, hold a job, maintain a marriage, find happiness. Continually blaming our parents is an excuse to quit working on ourselves. It's our choice to leave life-depleting anger at the altar, to let go of residual rage, and to move on to a new self.

I'm back in Oak Park, Illinois, to be one of the keynote speakers at the hundredth anniversary celebration of my hometown. Seated at my table is one of the event coordinators, a woman named Gina Orlando, who has taken an intense interest in the subject of this book. Her brown hair upswept in a twist, and wearing a short black dress, Orlando, forty-eight, is a hypnotherapist who says she has "spent my whole life trying to figure out who I am." This is a person who understood from the get-go growing up in an old-fashioned

Catholic family on the South Side of Chicago that she could not count on anyone else, not even her own parents, to make herself whole and healthy; that it was totally up to her to become her true self, a self she calls a "wounded healer." Here is her story:

I always felt pulled to the healing arts, and hypnosis is a wonderful field with so many possibilities to help people in significant ways. The goal of my work as a hypnotherapist is to help people move through their stuck stuff so they can get to their true self and create the life they want and deserve.

As my Italian grandmother always said, "Ev'rybody gotta some-a-ting." We all have stuff that keeps us from our true loving selves. In our culture we are oriented to talk therapy, which deals mostly with the conscious mind. You may become aware of your issues, but not necessarily free from them. I have been helped by talk therapy, by being heard and supported. But I never felt that I truly broke clear and free of my stuff until I went deeper with hypnotherapy.

My great life struggle has been to find my healing path, since I was determined to have light in my life. This process of excavating mind, body, and spirit has been so difficult at times, a journey through the dark night of the soul. What has helped me so much to move out of this darkness, both personally and professionally, was hypnosis. It gave me the support to break through to me.

Our True Self wants us to be our best selves. A person may keep on excess weight because of rage at a husband or father, padding as protection, or to push away lovers. To get to that part that is clearly loving, compassionate, and capable of true intimacy, you often need to peel away the layers and do some deep inner healing.

My own life situation thrust me on the path of the wounded healer, of trying to be healed myself. I was blessed to grow up in a loving extended middle-class family, but unfortunately one that did not protect me from a crazy, alcoholic, and abusive father. He had a demonic rage against women and I was his prime target. There were no bruises, only horrible threats of murder.

The daily verbal, mental, and emotional abuse caused very deep wounds. And the family system was, and is, in massive denial. Because I didn't get protection or validation for my outrage, the pain was enormous. Somehow I knew I had to rise above this situation. Somehow I had to find my own way.

Part of surrendering to your true self is having your real name. Unfortunately, my mother misnamed me, getting the ethnic slant on my name wrong. So my nickname growing up was Jeanie. I hated it. Every time that I heard someone call me that, I said to myself, "That is not my name. Why are they calling me that?" I was called Gina sometimes by my mother, but always by my Italian grandmother. When she said Gina, my whole body would relax and I'd say, "Yes, that's who I am." When I finally did claim my name, some family members were hurt, because to them, I was Jeanie. I felt so hurt by their anger. I am Gina Orlando.

My first memory of an intimate connection to God and

good, of knowing my place and path, comes from when I was only nineteen months old. But the memory is so clear. It was Easter, and my mother and I were walking out of church. She had recently given birth to my brother, and I had this wonderful feeling of having my mother to myself. I felt so pretty in my pink bonnet and pink coat, holding my mother's hand, hearing the wonderful organ music, seeing and smelling spring. All of a sudden I had this transcendent experience. I became part of everything good, one with God, one with my mother's love, one with the love of the universe and feeling so strongly that resurrection was my path. This experience seared every facet of my being with the sure knowledge that I am part of that goodness, that there are greater things out there to experience, that even though I would experience pain, I would not be the pain. It cut through the illusion of suffering. Because of this experience, although I am a spiritual seeker and a student of world religions, I still call myself a Christian mystic.

From the time I was very young, there was darkness coming from my father, which made it so that all light, joy, hope was snuffed out in our house at times. Alcoholism was only a small part of it; he suffered from serious mental and emotional disease. Yet although his darkness colored my life greatly, I refused to believe it was part of my core. My core is whole and happy and healthy. And so my life journey has been a quest to find that self that is full of light, my God self. I believe everyone has that self. So the work I do in hypnotherapy, helping people dissipate their darkness, is what I was truly meant to do. I know darkness all too well.

My mom and I were very close, she was a very loving mother, and I miss her dearly since she died in 1989. But I couldn't understand why she stayed with him. He would fly into rages, turn red, make threats of violence and murder, throw furniture, threaten to drive us and our car into a wall. I remember once when I was an adolescent, my father screamed at me when I had my period, calling me "a filthy pig, a filthy slut" at a time when I hadn't even kissed a boy. That kind of thing is devastating for a young woman. It can hit very deeply. And it is sexual abuse, even though it is not physical. The level of his rage and hatred toward me, and all women, was frightening and debilitating.

My mother didn't have the courage to leave him until I was about twenty-two years old. He had already broken her down. So my mother wasn't there for me in some ways, and my father wasn't there for me at all. This loss is a gift and a curse. The gift is that you are very independent and forced to rely on yourself. The curse is that you are not used to relying on or trusting someone else.

My father often said to me: "I feel sorry for the man who is going to marry you." That was the greatest hurt. I took these words in and did not feel pretty, desirable, or lovable to men. So I had a very difficult time with men and dating. I vowed to myself that I would never marry a man like my father. Yet there is an imprinting that goes on with this kind of abuse. Even though I aggressively wanted to avoid a man like this, I attracted them nonetheless, alcoholics and other men who were unavailable to me emotionally. This created such a sense of victimization.

Because of all of this, I didn't marry until I was forty, and my husband didn't want children. So I missed my opportunity to have children, which is a confusing loss in my life. Yet in the miraculous way that life has of directing us, there was a gift hidden inside the pain.

From my transcendent memory at church as a toddler in a pink Easter bonnet, I have continued on a spiritual search, and in 1982, I ended up at Unity Temple in Oak Park, a Unitarian Universalist church designed by Frank Lloyd Wright. There I coordinated and took part in wonderful layperson-led services for many years. In 1991, I coordinated a trilogy of services on men, women, and relationship issues. During one of these, I gave a five-minute sermon on my plight as a single woman in search for her true partner. I shared my difficult and dysfunctional past with men. I wore a gold pin that looked like a medal, calling it my badge of courage for being in the dating world for twenty-four years. I spoke of my abusive and alcoholic father. I explained my own personal healing process to get to a place of knowing who I was, what I wanted, and that I finally felt comfortable being alone. My future husband, Marty Berg, was in the congregation of three hundred people that day, "taking notes," as he later explained. He came up to me the next week and thanked me for my "honesty and openness" at the service. Marty had this great smile and great light and energy coming from him. I thought, "Who is this guy?"

That began a nice friendship; the romantic part wasn't there for a year. In the meantime, some of us from the Unity Temple created a ritual group which met once a month, when we would share our spiritual thoughts. I looked forward to Marty's turn, sensing some wonderful depth in him. And when Marty presented, I was blown away. One day someone rear-ended me and my new Honda Civic in a car accident, and I got whiplash. My car was totaled, and I needed a man to hug me and hold me. Of all the people I knew, all I could think of was calling Marty.

I got his recording with his gorgeous low bass voice, and I left a message, saying, "I need a back rub, a hug and man to say 'you can handle this.'" He called me back and said that he would love to get together. And that night he was so present for me, the light just really turned on. Within a month we both had this feeling that we were supposed to be married. After all my wounds about men all of my life, our relationship came from a very quiet place, a centered place, a peaceful place.

Of course even healthy relationships are imperfect. After seven years of marriage, we struggle deeply with very difficult issues, ones where old wounds touch old wounds. One of my struggles was to make peace that our marriage would be without children. On our first date, he said "I don't want children," and I thought that was an odd thing to say on a first date. So I knew what I was getting into, and I married for partnership, friendship, and love. But now that I'm shifting into menopause, there is grief for the children I will never have.

I never envisioned myself in a family of two. It's too small. In a family of two, you are always coming head to head with yourself and your broken places; sometimes it's too intense. But for someone who struggled for nearly fifty years to know herself, constantly coming head to head with who you are is probably a good thing. And I got a love beyond what I ever dreamed was possible from a man. His love has been one of the most amazing, healing forces in my life. Marty is real, honest, deep, sincere, kind, smart, and very funny. Through all of this crap around men, me, and sexuality, I have learned one very important thing. My sexuality is mine. It doesn't belong to anyone else—not to this culture, not to any church, not to my father, not to my old boyfriends, not even to my husband. My sexuality is for me, and I deserve pleasure, connection, and expression without shame, deprivation, or threats.

This man I married really grabs me on the level of soul. And I can't tell you how much I needed that, to trust a man. Part of my healing was confronting my father that he was an abuser. I gave him a last shot to create some resemblance of a healthy relationship. As expected, he did not take this opportunity for his own healing, and instead turned my family against me. His sisters sent our wedding pictures back to us.

My father and I have not spoken for going on ten years. He is in his dying process, and I do wonder what happens to souls who have a lot of darkness, how they move toward the light. I pray for the highest and best for him and wish him peace eternal. This is my letting go. I finally put him in God's hands and God's care. It's not my job to help him. It's not my job to change him. I cannot change other people. I can only change myself. Once you speak the truth your life will never be the same.

As Orlando painfully discovered, an ability to speak the truth comes from knowing the truth: That you and I are responsible for our own happiness. Her father hurt her deeply, but he did not destroy her. She discovered an unbreakable self within, a self of hope. Orlando speaks of letting go, of forgiveness, of finally coming to reside in a centered place, a peaceful place. We can blame others for our circumstances and choose despondency, or we can take responsibility, fully, for who we are at this moment, and live presently, thankfully, in peaceful surrender.

My kids are fed, the dishes are clean, and I sink into an Adirondack chair on the hill outside my kitchen. It's 6:36 P.M. and the crickets are twanging, and I'm woozy from the humidity. I think of my mother and father and all of our parents, and how children are formed into adults who form themselves. I think about the journey we all must take to grow, the lashes that wound, the lessons we learn, and the satisfaction that comes from making it through tunnels into the next self. Chuck is sawing wood for shelves, straddling the red brick steps, and I smell the pine dust and fill up on my life. I couldn't be more satiated than now, on this Thursday night. I want to hold on forever to this moment of light, every nuance of its simplicity and majesty. This is all I have, I know, this sliver of time.

Nothing slams you into the moment with more ferocity, and appreciation, than being around people who have a terminal illness, folks who are hungry to devour everything around them, people who don't waste time. They know with resounding clarity what really matters and who really counts. We have much to learn from these courageous friends and family members who understand mortality, and do not fear it. They live with urgency and passion. Gary Caruso, forty-four, was diagnosed five years ago with a rare cancer called adenoid cystic carcinoma, which runs from the palate to the base of the brain near the hypothalamus and pituitary gland. His doctors can't tell him whether he will live several more months or decades. Yet rather than hover in fear, Caruso feels stronger, and ironically more joyful, than ever.

The former deputy executive director of President Clinton's presidential advisory committee on Gulf War veterans' illnesses, Caruso now works as a freelance strategic consultant. Outside of work, the only people he spends time with are those he wants to see; he feels no compulsion to fulfill obligations for purely social reasons. He has come to know that real power comes from a few loving relationships, not lots of powerful acquaintances.

Unsure of how much time he has, Caruso today finds happiness in puttering around his house and reading war histories. When I think of putting things off until the time is right, Caruso reminds me that this is the right time. Here is his story:

Every doctor has told me that with this type of cancer, you will always live with it; you never get to a stage where after five or ten or fifteen years you are pronounced cancer-free. It's the nature of this particular kind of cell, historically it has an enormously high recurrence rate, and it tends to metastasize elsewhere in the body, either in the brain or in the lungs. Even in ten years you could be walking around, saying everything is great, then boom, it shows up somewhere else in your body.

For that reason alone I will never wake up and say "Hallelujah, I'm free of this condition," because I would never want to set myself up for that kind of disappointment.

I'll never forget the look on my surgeon's face when he found out there were still positive margins on the original tumor. He thought he got all of it. He, along with one of the premier head and neck surgeons at Sloan-Kettering, kept on reiterating how "this is one of the most tricky cancers that we have to deal with." The other irony of this disease is that only 150 to 200 people are diagnosed with it each year in the United States—it's that rare. So there are no clinical trials like there would be with breast or prostate cancer, where hundreds of thousands of people are diagnosed with it each year. So I have had to learn to live with extreme uncertainty.

Because of all that has happened to me, I have reduced my life to a very simple existence. Everything in my life now has to be functional and purposeful. I'm much more laid-back than I ever have been, and more important, at peace with myself. I no longer have regrets about things that used to keep me up at night. Today I rarely get angry about anything bad that happens.

You can say that I've reached that zone, that level where I'm comfortable with who I am as a person. I'm not getting up and saying, "Gee, if I only studied premed in college, I could have gone to medical school," or any other regrets or doubts. This may sound strange, but I'm more content now than ever.

For too long in my life I tried to measure myself against my father—a man who graduated high school at sixteen, was president of both his high school and college classes; a man who had skipped two grades, went to law school at night in

three years, got his master's in teaching; a supremely intelligent and accomplished person. He was a type A personality;
both he and his brothers were the smartest kids around, the
best at what they did. As a kid growing up, I knew the image
of my father and my uncles, who were brilliant do-gooders. I
remember being very self-critical in the past; if you got a 99
instead of a 100, it was a failure. I used to always have this
thing about perfection. If it wasn't perfect, then I was a failure.
And now I don't feel that way anymore. I do what I can do,
and that's it. And I don't judge myself anymore, particularly
against other people.

I don't think in terms of life goals. There are some places
I haven't been where I want to go, such as New Zealand, Australia, the South Pacific. But those are minor things. There are
no material things in life that I want: I would never want to be
rich because I feel material wealth can have a detrimental
impact on your life. The greatest gift any person can con-
tribute to life is helping others, even if that means just being a
decent friend, neighbor, or human being.

I know this sounds a little trite, but in its most basic
form, people just want to be free to express themselves, to be
respected by their peers, their family, their friends, to be
understood by others for the person they truly are. Getting
derailed by this medical trauma has actually helped put my
life more on track. It added a tranquility I never had. I sometimes still get angry at people, but it's for a very short period
of time.

I haven't really dated that much since my cancer was
diagnosed, but that's the other part of it. You get to a certain

point and you look for something different in a mate. I find myself looking back at the way I was as a stupid teenage boy and everything to me was appearance. I was at a baseball game yesterday, at Camden Yards in Baltimore, and I watched teenagers interact. It's almost like the TV show Animal Kingdom, *you can watch the mating going on. You see that it is purely hormonal, physical and immediate. Over the years I have found myself much more attracted to intelligent people, people with good hearts.*

Several years ago, I made a conscious decision to stay away from politics. I watched the political process slowly change since I first got involved almost twenty-five years ago. I worked for both John Glenn and Jimmy Carter in the late seventies and early eighties. I spent a lot of time with John Glenn on the road and I just knew I would never be able to work for another person I so admired and respected. His character, beliefs, and devotion to our country are extraordinary; Hollywood would have a hard time creating a man like John Glenn.

Unfortunately, in Washington you tend to have a lot of trivial relationships because people are interested in what you can do for them, so they make nice, and you become the person-of-the-moment in their lives, you become a good contact. In a strange way, Washington politics is a metaphor for the movie Lord of the Flies: *Innocence is exchanged in the quest for survival, power, and influence—while the selfless more often than not symbolize the befallen boar.*

My own struggle with cancer helped drive home this point: When I got sick, all my nonpolitical friends came rushing to my door. The people I knew in my political life, most of them filtered away. Since completing my treatment program I consciously decided to live a much more solitary life, and I have a sense of tranquility that most healthy people cannot know: There is a permanence to my medical condition, a permanence which gives people like me an insight into a part of life which most people fear: death.

Most people don't know if we're going to die of a heart attack or a stroke or get hit by a truck or die in a plane crash. In a sense, I know what's going to happen, and that in turn has removed many of the fears most of us live with on a daily basis. Today I can unequivocally say I have absolutely no fear of dying. Maybe you can say that there is a transition point in everyone's life—a threshold or Rubicon that everyone must cross to reach a higher mental and emotional state. I guess I look at the world differently today than I did five years ago. I see people getting upset over senseless issues; people rushing to get somewhere; people setting unrealistic goals in their lives, and I say, for what? Some days I think I'm just the luckiest person in the world for being able to see what's really important in life and what's not. Never again will you find me racing around trying to get somewhere I really don't want to go to.

Over the last several years, I've donated a ton of things to the Salvation Army, I just went through all my closets and realized I don't need that coat, I don't need that suit, I don't need that tie. There are people who have so little and can really use what hangs in most of our closets. Today my world is less cluttered than it used to be. You can say I've prepared for a quick and organized exit to life. I've watched too many people die and how it becomes a burden to one's family. If that day comes, and it will, I want to make it as easy as possible for everyone around me. It is really a very loving and respectful thing to do for the most important people in your life.

I do not put off things anymore that I want to do. My father has a cousin who is ninety-one years old and lives in Vermont. He's the oldest living cousin in the family and I haven't seen him in thirty years. And I wanted to see him because he was a link to my past. One day I just got in my car and literally drove up the East Coast to see him. He was so thrilled that I would drive over five hundred miles just to visit him. He pulled out a worn shoe box and showed me some old family photos. I saw a picture of my great-grandmother, whom I had never before laid eyes on. It was taken in 1901, and that one picture sent me on a voyage to trace my past. I wanted to know everything about every aspect of my family. I wanted to know who they were, where they lived, what they did, and what kind of people they were. On my computer, I have started keeping a record of everything I learn about my family.

When this first happened, I went through this introspective period, and asked myself: Why me? Why did this have to happen? Then it becomes something of a watershed in your life. At first you keep on thinking that this is the worst thing that can ever happen to any human being. Then you start to realize how the experience changes you for the good. Soon I started to see that in some respects this is the best thing that ever happened. Cancer acts like a filter; you no longer waste time on meaningless issues, you completely eject trivial things from your psyche that just occupy space and time.

Everything I do now has to have a sense of purpose,

whether it's reading a book or going on-line on the computer. There has to be meaning to it, as opposed to "I'm going to sit here and watch television just because I'm going to run the clock out on my life." I've also changed my work habits. I used to be one of those people who would take pride in working eighteen hours a day. Not anymore. Every day at lunch, for example, I go off by myself and I do a crossword puzzle. When I get home at night, I love to cook dinner and then read something on the Civil War or World War II history.

I'm never alone anymore, even when there isn't another human being within a hundred miles of me. I've found that place in the center of myself—a place we all have but most people have never been.

TRAVELING TO FIND YOURSELF

Gary Caruso talks about residing in his center, a place that goes where he goes. Many people travel to the farthest distance on a map to find what Caruso discovered in his own heart. You too can find yourself anywhere you happen to be. You can be in your kitchen, cleaning strawberries, listening to the rain beating on your window. Answers to looming life questions—Who am I? What is my mission?—aren't in other states or other countries.

I'm buying a malachite and silver bracelet for my aunt Gloria in a Native American crafts shop in Arizona. The shopper behind me at the cash register asks where I am from. I tell her I live an hour from Washington and an hour from Baltimore. She says that she spent her girlhood in Napa Valley, used to live just outside Washington in Bethesda, Maryland, when she was briefly married; has lived in Arizona for going on six years, but where she really wants to be is in Utah. I ask her why she would want to move from Arizona, a state people move to, not from. She said that what she was looking for was not in Arizona. I asked her what she was hoping to find.

My husband signals me from across the store to stop talking and pay—his hand motion for this is to take an index finger and slash it across his throat—so we could route our fidgety children out of a store where there were lots of breakable items. But I am drawn to this woman, I've been this woman before, searching all over for something intangible. She looks hard at me; she is about fifty with a very tanned face and very blonde hair, in very tight black leather pants. Then she says, "I don't know what I'm looking for. When I find it, I will know."

I wanted to say so much to her, this stranger holding a strand of silver and coral beads. But Chuck was in the car with the engine running, and what could I tell her? Nobody can advise anyone else to stay in Arizona and not go to Utah, warning her that once she gets to Utah she may want to move to Alaska, then still not be satisfied. Eventually we all figure out that a place only gives us temporary peace, that sustained peace comes from within. We all know people who flit from flower to flower, sniffing out perfection, something that doesn't exist.

On our trip through Arizona, we spend two days in Sedona, trekking through this town of red rocks and old hippies. I am compelled to buy a booklet called *The Sedona Vortex Experience*, written by local authors Gaia Lamb and Shinana Naomi Barclay. The cover line reads: "How to tune in, find your personal power place, and take the magic home." A vortex in Sedona, which growth-groupies began to view as one of the major power points on the planet some two decades ago, means a spiraling cone of energy that swirls through your consciousness. And lore has it, there are some major vortexes to be tapped into here.

I sit in an outdoor café filled with men with ponytails and women in halter tops, and began to read in my vortex guide how, if you "center and ground yourself" on a flat rock at one of Sedona's highest power points, such as Schnebly Hill or the Airport Mesa, then "allow your hands and arms to stir, circle, move, pulse, and flow in and out like the movements of a jellyfish," you will begin to feel energy under your armpits that gives you the sensation you are flying like an eagle through "cosmic soup." I look at a barefoot man playing a folk guitar and chewing tobacco next to me, and the fiery rock formations sculpted into mystical and sexual shapes in the near distance. The sounds of the adjacent creek rush through me. Without flapping my wings, yet imagining an eagle soaring in me, I was swimming in some serious cosmic soup right in this café. Soaking in the cedar and pine smells and the last drop of a Corona, I liked this me in Sedona, a me like the waitress of the middle-70s who worked in a halter top in a restaurant called the New Varsity in Palo Alto. I felt a total lifetime in this moment; was I in a vortex?

I read on: "You are as vast as your conscious awareness can extend. . . . Look to the horizon beyond the Red Rocks . . . extend your consciousness out to the horizon. Look up at the clouds floating in the great blue sky. You are that vast. Breathe deeply and extend your consciousness to one cloud, then another, and another. Then extend into the outer space of the blue sky and/or to the moon.

"Why are we so awed when we look into the starry heavens on a clear night?" the chapter continues. "Because we are that vast . . . Experience your vastness, then return your conscious awareness to your heart center. Feel your vastness there. Place your hands over your heart center, breathe deeply and anchor this new feeling of magnificence into your being."

I swirled out of there feeling young, light, and strange, picturing the vast magnificence of my being. As I walked toward the crowded downtown shops where I was meeting my family, I kept hearing an echo: "Be vast, be vast." When people come back from a great vacation, whether it's skiing or camping or lying at the lip of the sea, much of what they say revolves around the theme: You could see forever. It was just me and the mountain, or me and the ocean, or me and the stars. Quite simply, they expand. That sense of vastness tends to swallow petty anxieties, petty gripes, petty selves, and fills you with serenity; indeed, it takes you into a new magnificence of being, a place where you aren't thinking, you simply are. To be aware of vastness is true cosmic consciousness, a genuine realization of the enormity of the cosmos.

We live in a rural community with low-rise buildings, and the sky is gigantic and the bay goes on forever and I get lost in dreams and nature all the time. But coming back from Sedona, I am able to get lost a lot faster, because I now focus on enlarging my self by fixating on a star and throwing my consciousness out there. When you are feeling glum or small, throw your consciousness upward, in the direction of heaven. Get your arms around all that space, let it fill you up. The grandeur will dwarf the little stuff gnawing and gnashing inside of you. In the country, the skyline is uncluttered by structures and pollution, and heaven is easier to get to; in the city, to reach heaven, find the highest terrace and beam toward the sky. You are suddenly on vacation, without surreal red rocks or the perfume of pine and cedar found in Northern Arizona. All you need is your imagination and an open heart.

When I usher in silence and space, any music I'm listening to feels as if it is playing inside my soul, vibrating within, instead of being played around me. In a wide and empty self, an entire orchestra can perform and I get lost in it, and I get found in it, and I am home.

In more than forty years of visits there, Arizona never fails to clear me out, to get me lost and found. Yet I've learned to take Arizona with me wherever I am, picturing my self glowing like the desert sunset, a beacon that lives in me and not in a place. An eternal light resides in your own soul, and it can make the 10-degree, pewter days of winter seem a lot more tolerable. It can burn while you're washing a sinkful of dirty dishes. It can calm you when phones keep ringing and email banks are crammed with eighty-seven dispatches. Your light can ease the grind of ordinary life.

Sometimes at night, when the moon is full, I stand outside and I stretch my arms out as far as I can and let the moon hit me right in my heart. It can be any size moon, it's the light that I absorb, right to my core, and I imagine it flashing like a diamond.

"All of us have a supreme jewel in the depths of our hearts, and we have come into life for no other purpose than to discover this jewel here on earth while we are alive," writes Eknath Easwaran in *Climbing the Blue Mountain: A Guide for the Spiritual Journey*. Our lives pulsate with technological distractions that yank us away from our vortex of light, our center of calm. We must build souls that are strong enough to tune out the yammer, by flexing not just our muscles, but our spiritual lives. We need to reach a plateau where we don't need breathtaking scenery to make us feel tranquil. Listening to folk guitar in a Sedona café at the foot of a mountain next to a gushing creek infused me with a surge of heart and soul energy. But I keep figuring out ways to own that surge when I'm back in my office, with a stack of bills and a mountain of mundane tasks to do.

Vacations come and go. You don't stay in Tahiti, you

just visit Tahiti. It's the peaks and reservoirs inside us that are the resources that give us ultimate satisfaction. We take our vortexes with us, our sun centers go where we go. My New York friend Leslie is just back from Italy, she can't stay away from that country that makes her believe in reincarnation: "Italy is home; I know it as if I've been there for centuries." When Leslie strokes Italian marble, smooth and cold on her palms, she experiences a Proustian moment, a swatch in time in which, through a smell, an object or an image, one is transported, vividly, to the original moment of encounter, which for Leslie seems like an earlier life. The term comes from Marcel Proust's *Remembrance of Things Past*, a scene in which the protagonist tastes a morsel of a sweet madeleine cake soaked in tea, then promptly swirls into a sublime reverie of another life, his life, whose life?

"No sooner had the warm liquid, and the crumbs with it, touched my palate than a shudder ran through my whole body," writes Proust. ". . . this new sensation having had on me the effect which love has of filling me with a precious essence; or rather this essence was not in me, it was myself. I had ceased now to feel mediocre, accidental, mortal. Whence could it have come to me, this all powerful joy? I was conscious that it was connected with the taste of tea and cake, but that it infinitely transcended those savours. . . . Whence did it come?"

He combs his memory to pinpoint exactly what the sweet tea triggered, who he was then, where he was. Suddenly he sees himself as a boy with his aunt Leonie, who used to give him a madeleine dipped in lime-flower tea on Sunday mornings, and he is awash in childhood remembrances: an old gray house, a pond, a garden, country roads, waterlilies, the parish church, and the whole of the town of Combray, where she lived. All this "sprang into being, town and gardens alike," from a tiny taste of tea.

Proustian moments come to me constantly in Tucson, from touching turquoise, from dusty trails, from cactus jutting out like giant lollipops, from an inexplicable cry of the soul. When I'm riding a horse in Sabino Canyon, I am four and six and twelve again. I have a clear picture of me as someone else, a woman with brown skin and silver bracelets and long braids. In February in Maryland, when the skies over the Severn River are not cosmic soup, but like virulent chowder, I locate my sun center and let the beams shoot through me. I feel the lope of the horse, an ancient contentment.

People travel to the outer edges of the world looking for their sun centers, and they may find a place, an Arizona, that sets their soul ablaze. But we don't stay on vacation; we live in our homes, we live in ourselves. So we need to figure out a way to find ourselves without moving.

"Over one long holiday weekend more than five hundred precious lives may be lost on the highways, mostly due to the frantic desire to find happiness somewhere other than where we are," notes Eknath Easwaran in *Climbing the Blue Mountain*. "And the state of California in which I live leads the list of casualties. Yosemite Park often seems as crowded as Market Street in San Francisco. Lake Tahoe is like the Financial District at noon. All this rushing about, which leads to such casualties and such sorrow, is a kind of compulsive pursuit, looking outside us in the belief that that is where joy and fulfillment hide."

Blasé about her routine in the hometown she had lived in for twenty-seven years, Molly left for Australia and New Zealand for a year, with no family there, just a short list of friends of friends as contacts. I interviewed her when she returned from crisscrossing the world, and as she puts it, for all she uncovered, she may as well have just camped out in her backyard.

An earthy blonde in overalls, Molly advises other like-minded wanderers to have a more focused idea than she had of what they're looking for when they leave behind everything they love, load up a backpack, and head off for an open-ended adventure.

I was restless and looking for a different way of life. I'd been living in this small town my whole life, and I was bored with my job as a manager of a health food store. And I thought by stepping into the unknown I could create a new life.

It was an open-ended journey; I knew when and where I was going, but I didn't know exactly when I would return. I went down there with a work visa, but I had no job lined up and I didn't know anyone, except friends of friends I had contacted. Frankly, I didn't even do that much research on Australia. One January day, I just landed in Sydney. So I was completely disoriented when I got there, to say the least. I'd just spent twenty-two hours in the air, then I land in this other hemisphere.

Honestly, my fantasy fizzled before I even left the States. My first flight went from the East Coast to Los Angeles, and I had a long layover there. So I took a cab from the airport to Santa Monica, to sit on the beach for a while. As I sat there I'm thinking: "What are you doing? You just said goodbye to everyone you love, for what?" It was an excruciatingly lonely moment. I mean, I could have just driven a couple of hours to New Jersey if this was how getting away from it all was going to be like.

I sat there and became fearful about this adventure: When was I going to connect with another person I could feel close to again? Was I going to find work? I started questioning all these things I hadn't allowed myself to think about while I was busy planning the trip.

My original plan was to stay in Australia for six weeks, travel and see the sights, then go find work in New Zealand. Early in my trip, though, I started to realize that this great fantasy escape I'd been planning for months might be shorter than expected and not turn out to be so great. You fantasize about Australia and New Zealand in your mind; you imagine the open spaces and the beaches and handsome, athletic men surfing. And it is beautiful there, but immediately I felt like this was not the place of my dreams. Really, I didn't know what I was looking for. All I knew was that I was twenty-seven years old and something was missing from my life and that I was going to find it.

Most women my age were taking very traditional steps. After getting a good job they were eager to get married. And that just wasn't me. I never have been one to follow a traditional path, I had no marriage prospects, and I needed to enlarge my world.

I did end up meeting people in Australia that I felt connected to, and we did a lot of great tours. I took in the most incredible natural beauty that I probably ever will. I stepped foot on remote islands in the South Pacific that felt completely undiscovered. I went into the Outback with a group of eight people in an old Land Rover. Imagine driving for many days and seeing the same open and barren landscape. It was really like being on the road to nowhere.

It was humbling being in such a small group of people in the vastness of open land. Animals and red rock formations outnumbered us by a long shot. We were in a land that was so unpolluted by development that at night it felt like you could see every star and planet in the universe. I went scuba diving and snorkeling in the Great Barrier Reef. Swimming alongside brilliantly colored schools of fish made me feel again like a small part of something larger.

And there are the unforgettable disappointments. One of my first big letdowns was trying to find a job. I had gone for this interview with a New Zealand magazine, and I gave them all these story ideas and they said, "Great, we love your ideas." But then they told me "Well, we can't afford to pay you, but we'd really like for you to do some work for us." At this point I couldn't afford to work for free. I went overseas with only a few thousand American dollars, and without work, even living very simply, you can go through that pretty fast.

I met a lot of people who had spent the last few years traveling, constantly moving from place to place. And I realized that this kind of life just wasn't for me; I need connectiveness and I need roots and I need to be around good friends. The fantasy of what I did really started peeling away. And I made some wrong choices, particularly one relationship.

I met this man who was traveling the world in a sailboat and he was looking for someone to come along. I told him I might be interested in crewing. And he was pretty honest with me, saying, "Well, I'm not necessarily only looking for crew." He was looking for somebody special for play. And I just thought, "I'm not going there." We kept up an email exchange over the course of several weeks and then I thought that maybe this was something I should try. I wasn't really doing anything else, I might as well go sailing with him.

About the sixth day at sea, things started going bad. I knew I had made the wrong decision. I saw this other personality coming forward—cold, very snappy. I stayed on the boat for a month and it was torture. I would read books. I would talk to dolphins before I would talk to him. One month of an ice-cold silence on a boat nearly did me in. He had the classic traveler mentality, a guy who is looking and looking for something, very discontented with the life he has. A loner.

When I got off his boat I was a real mess. I had pinkeye in both eyes. My face was all broken out because I had gotten eye drops with sulfur and I'm allergic to sulfur. I had my twentieth bad cold of the trip. I was broke, and not even interested in looking for work again. And it's blustery winter weather on the island. I said, "That's it. I'm going home." I'd seen enough of this country and now I wanted to see my home after five months away.

When my parents first saw me walking off the plane, they said in dismay: "What happened to you?" My eyes were still messed up and my body was just so physically stressed. I went to the end of the world to find out that my life was good at home. I never realized how important friends and family are to me, how lucky I am to have these people in my life. I realized that I don't have to move to New York or to California or somewhere else because what I want and need I had already started here, it was something inside of me.

You know, I don't regret doing it, but at the same time I should have asked myself deeper questions before I left, like "What exactly am I looking for?", something beyond a travel experience. I was not prepared for the sheer loneliness. I did experience great beauty, and I love challenging myself, but there were points where I just felt, "God, everything I love is so far away, everything that's important to me."

One of the toughest things about the experience was coming back and doing the same thing I had left doing. Ultimately I did switch jobs. The adventurer in me still says, "I've got to do more, I've got to be more," but after my travels, I see now that I am a person who needs to be in close proximity to those I love. I also realized that you don't get answers to life questions in a sudden epiphany. You get answers in pieces on the longer journey through all of your life.

AGING WITH FINESSE

Molly is still young, but she has a mature take on who she is and what she requires to be happy. I often ask people old enough to be my grandparents to give me their secrets on how to live long and happily. My survey is hardly far flung and longitudinal, but if I've talked to forty people in their eighties and beyond, I can tell you that 99 percent of them listed the number-one reason they're still alive is that they have kept themselves engaged in work or hobbies they love. The findings of my small survey are corroborated by author Neenah Ellis, who takes a penetrating look at what it takes to live a very long time in her new book, *If I Live to Be 100*, based on her National Public Radio series *One Hundred Years of Stories*. I heard the author on NPR, and when asked if the centenarians she interviewed shared any significant traits, Ellis replied: "They are all optimistic, resilient, and are passionate about something beyond themselves."

A few years back I asked Elizabeth Campbell, then ninety-six, and the founder of WETA television, the Washington area Public Broadcasting Service, what it felt like to be inching toward a hundred. Without pausing, she said matter-of-factly: "I never thought about how old I was. When things came up, I just did them, honey." At the same time, I also spoke to Dr. Leila Denmark, then a hundred, who was treating up to thirty patients a day in her pediatrician's office in Alpharetta, Georgia. Denmark, who was still practicing at a hundred and three, told me that she never tried any of the anti-aging elixirs that boomers young enough to be her grandchildren are gulping down. After seventy years on the job, Denmark huffed, "What for?" when asked if she takes megavitamins.

"I don't think you need a bit of those new things," she scoffed at the mention of newfangled supplements like ginkgo biloba, an extract from the leaves of the ginkgo tree taken to bolster memory.

"I just eat three simple meals a day, protein in every meal, eggs, lean meat, beans, or nuts," Denmark told me. "If you want to live a long time, you have to eat right, and you have to love what you're doing. I have been in practice since 1928, and I have always loved going to work."

Love what you're doing is also Campbell's advice to those who want to live long and live well. She said an ongoing passion for people and education has been what fuels her over the years. She started the Greater Washington Educational Telecommunications Association in 1953, now one of the largest-producing PBS stations.

"I think most people can live a long time if you have a job you want to go to and people you are close to," said Campbell. "I've always had work to live for, and I've always had people who needed me. It is terribly important to wake up in the morning and know there are people out there to whom you make a difference."

Their straightforward strategies for maintaining vigor and clarity are echoed in the scientific conclusions of a decade-long study of 1,350 seniors conducted by the

MacArthur Foundation Research Network on Successful Aging. In the book *Successful Aging,* which documents the study, authors John W. Rowe and Robert L. Kahn found that the key factors contributing to mental and physical functioning in later years are social connectedness, exercise, and engaging in productive activities.

Witnessing the resurrection of Fleetwood Mac, still gyrating and sexy at fifty-plus, has fanned all our fantasies of growing hotter as we age. The reality is that the massive block of baby boomers, which started turning sixty-five in 2001, has got a lot more time to live their dreams. In 1900, life expectancy at birth in the United States was forty-seven years; today people over seventy-five are the fastest-growing segment of the population.

While the boomers can rightly claim to have shaken up politics, culture and gender roles, the anti-aging revolution is clearly not our creation. By the time Ponce de Leon set out to discover the fountain of youth in 1512 and found Florida instead, time had already been considered an enemy for centuries. Since the ancient days of Methuselah, allegedly age 969, people have conjured up all sorts of radical ideas to extend life and charge the libido.

Youth-seekers have eaten tiger gonads and the bone marrow of lions. They have received injections into their muscles of crushed testicles from young dogs and guinea pigs. Scariest of all, around the time of World War I, a Russian scientist named Serge Voronoff set up shop on the French Riviera and started grafting genitalia from monkeys onto men, under their own testicles. This last experiment was a long-running disaster. The monkey testicle experiments are particularly disturbing because while people suffered horrendous side effects, the hype was so great customers still kept coming to Voronoff for some thirty years.

While researchers dissent on the efficacy and dangers of anti-aging potions and hormone replacement therapy, they do agree that the most successful agers have key characteristics in common: They continue to learn, feel in charge of their lives, and exercise. Perhaps the most important clue to be uncovered on how we age is that lifestyle changes more than heredity, made even in later years, are the primary determinant of longevity.

In short, you can teach an old dog new tricks.

"Our most surprising finding is that we are responsible for our own old age," according to Dr. John Rowe, coauthor of the book *Successful Aging*. "Only about 30 percent of aging is inherited."

For the PBS series called *Stealing Time* that aired in 1999, John Palfreman, one of the show's producers, buried himself in state-of-the-art studies on the cognitive aspects of aging. His reporting revealed that brains do not have to wither with time.

"It used to be very widely believed that brain cells died off progressively from your twenties onward," Palfreman says. "Yet a whole lot of research is now showing that some brain regions in humans do not have significant cell death as you age." Rather, as the brain is stimulated, it sprouts new projections called dendrites, which grow like limbs on trees.

As you keep feeding your mind, these cells continue to grow throughout the entire life cycle.

While an aging brain can sprout new branches, so can a sweating body sprout muscles in later years. One classic Boston study done in the early 1990s tracked nursing home residents as old as ninety-eight who did sets of exercises on weight machines three times a week for eight weeks. Results showed muscle strength to increase an average of 74 percent, and their walking speed increased 50 percent.

Washingtonian Evelyn Stefansson Nef decided to give herself a flat tummy for her eightieth birthday, so she signed on with a personal trainer. Nine years later, she is still working out on the treadmill and pumping iron. After several abdominal surgeries, Nef can never have a washboard stomach, but it is tighter and stronger, as is the rest of her. When she started working out, she could hardly lift her arm. With a full-scale fitness program, Nef was able to lift her leg to her ear and do 350 sit-ups in a row.

"And I can dance all night," says Nef. "I love to tango."

That she would become a fitness fanatic as an octogenarian didn't surprise anyone who has watched Nef unfold over the years. In earlier days, she used to trek through the Arctic with her late explorer husband, Vilhjalmur Stefansson, and at the age of sixty she went back to school to become a psychotherapist. She describes herself as a person who "always strives to do better in whatever I am doing," and she advises young people to do the same if they want to live long and well. Now eighty-nine, Nef just published her memoirs: *Finding My Way: The Autobiography of an Optimist.*

Ray Harrison, the owner of Annapolis Personal Training, is sixty-eight and rock hard and always up and running, starting with clients at 6:30 A.M. He says the most exciting results he sees are in people over sixty, grandparents who come in "stooped over," and after a few months of strengthening their core muscles with weights are standing tall, with zeal and "sparkle in their eyes."

"Moving your body on a regular basis gets you back in the game," says Harrison. "Hey, we're not going to make you twenty-one again, but if you start exercising and you are seventy or eighty, you can get your quality of life back. I'm sixty-eight and I feel fifty. I have two sons, the oldest is forty-nine, and I can do more than they can do. I can lift more weights, I have more energy, and I think I have a better outlook on life. Really, I still think like a twenty-one-year-old, which is dangerous.

"If you're getting older and feeling a lull in your life, it is amazing what we can do with your older body," adds Harrison. "After sixty, your mind starts playing a game with you: It tells you 'I can't do that. That's not what a sixty-year-old does.' The truth is, you can do it. If you train and keep at it and are in good health, you can do what a thirty-five-year old can do."

My husband's grandmother, Mattie Anthony, has never bench pressed weights or shelled out the fifty bucks an hour it takes for personal training. They don't have those perks in her country hometown on the Corsica River in Maryland. Yet she believes that muscles have memory, and the fact she drove her body hard all her life has kept her vigorous at the age of ninety-seven. None of her childhood friends are alive, and she outlived her son and his wife, my husband's parents. Her health has been generally very good; she breezed through hip-replacement surgery and the insertion of a pacemaker.

As a young girl, Mattie used to help her father as he plowed the family's farm in nearby Sudlersville. For recreation, she spent afternoons playing hours of baseball with her first cousin, who lived on the farm across the road. That boy was Jimmy Foxx, who was drafted by the Philadelphia Athletics and became one of the greatest sluggers in baseball history. As a young woman, Anthony rode horseback through rough woods to the one-room schoolhouse where she taught grades one through seven. After she retired from teaching at the age of sixty-five, she kept "bending and pulling and weeding" in her garden in which she raised her own vegetables. And she traveled the world, through Scandinavia, Japan, New Zealand, and China, and into the heart of the Alps.

"Had I just gone home and sat down after I retired I wouldn't be here today," says Anthony, a great-grandmother of thirteen. "All of my life I have never stopped moving. The people I know who stopped aren't around anymore."

We call this woman Granny and she stayed with us for a couple of days recently. I took her shopping to the department store Hechts and to T.J. Maxx, and she bought lots of new clothes, including a shocking pink suit. As we were driving home, bulging bags in the backseat, Granny started laughing, then said, "Well, I don't have any place to go and wear all these new things. But I'm going to wear them every day and just enjoy looking at myself in the mirror."

Most of us get new clothes because we want to present our best face to the world. Granny's joy is in simply wearing them for herself; they make her feel good as she sits in her sun-splashed reading room, where she devours historical novels and watches birds. I've known this woman for sixteen years, and she has never let herself go. I've never seen Granny in a housedress. I've never seen her without her makeup on. She still goes to the hairdresser once a week, on Fridays. And she lives alone. We should all grow old with grace and with something to do, leaving us no time for self-pity.

One of the highlights of teaching college journalism is bringing my students to the *Washington Post* to hear from Ben Bradlee, the longtime executive editor of the newspaper. When he stepped down from the top post in 1991, he was named vice-president-at-large. As Bradlee speaks about his colorful past, the students are as hushed as I ever see them, enchanted by the arrestingly handsome veteran of the news business who is larger than life in his presence and experiences. He documents this life in his bestselling memoir *A Good Life,* which tells of his six-month bout with polio at age fourteen, graduation from Harvard, his three and half years of naval service on a destroyer in the South Pacific during World War II, a close relationship with President John F. Kennedy, three marriages that produced four children, and leading the *Post* through its unraveling of Watergate, the biggest political scandal in American history.

The fit and energetic Bradlee still goes to the office nearly every day, yet his priority is no longer the mad scramble for news. Rather, his primary focus is his family—his wife, writer Sally Quinn, and their son Quinn, a bright and charismatic college freshman who has weathered physical and learning challenges and is now thriving. As Bradlee describes Quinn in *A Good Life*, a child who had five-and-a-half-hour open heart surgery by the time he was three months old:

> *His body had been unseamed, then closed with more than eighty stitches, and penetrated by more tubes and wires than I could count. He was fighting for his every breath, eyes tight shut. . . .*
>
> *How does an infant learn to fight that hard? Through tribulations that defied understanding—seizure disorders, speech difficulties, and learning disabilities—a valiant young man has emerged. . .*

The last time my class visited Bradlee, he told us: "There comes a point in a person's life when you look back and wonder if your life made any sense." Struck by that comment, I asked him if I could come back alone and talk to him about his climb down from executive editor of the *Washington Post* to a man content these days to just have the title of Dad and to tool around his 200 acres of land on the St. Mary's River in southern Maryland.

Here is Ben Bradlee at eighty-one, the raspy-voiced

legend who epitomizes resilience, optimism, and passion, the three qualities researchers believe to be the secrets to aging well:

At my age, you do question your life, and you do admit to any kind of failure. I'm not totally proud of everything. I mean, I wasn't very good at the marriage business. It took me a while to get the hang of that. But I don't believe for a life to make sense that you have to be all about success.

I've been in the newspaper business for a long time, and journalism has always been very important in my life. In looking back, I see that it was always a goal to be involved in something I felt passionate about, and this was it. I have never doubted whether I was in the right business. I love this business. In many ways, I was married to the newspaper, and that didn't help my first two marriages. Breaking news excites me on every level, from messes in the White House to John Bobbitt getting his tally-whacker whacked off by his wife.

Working at a newspaper—this is my real self. Even now, my relationship with the Washington Post *is umbilical. I still come here almost every day. And I don't have to look for things to do. I make speeches, I'm a sounding board for editors and reporters. I'm very engaged with this place. I stay connected because it feels right, it has always felt right. And it is a marriage in the sense that it's a deep, personal, satisfying bond.*

The pinnacle, of course, was Watergate, and that's vaguely discouraging to think that you peaked thirty years ago. But historically, there was never a news story that really had this impact until September 11. Everyone around the world knew about Watergate and Woodward and Bernstein, they knew about me.

But I don't miss that. No, I don't miss that at all. Because I never felt like that person. I never woke up and looked at myself in the mirror and said, "You powerful son of a bitch, you can do anything." What has dominated my life for the last twenty years, and really forms who I am, is my son Quinn. He graduated from high school with honors, and that was unbelievable. I was in heaven. He dominates both Sally's and my life because we will always need to nurture him and to protect him and to give him the confidence that those children lack.

But he's doing great, he's doing so well he fools people; you don't pick up right away on his disabilities, provided you don't talk quantum mechanics with him. He's good-looking and he loves people. I'm so proud of that kid. Really, Quinn changed my life.

In my other marriages, I cheated my kids. I wasn't around while they were growing up. At one point, when Ben was young, I wasn't even in the same country for a year. He is now deputy managing editor of the Boston Globe *(on leave to write a book about Ted Williams). It's just fantastic for him, and for me. But by the time Quinn came along in 1982, although I was still editor of the* Post, *it wasn't that frenetic scramble as it was during Watergate and other eras. I never felt like I had the job done, but I felt that I was on top of the job. I had more time on my hands.*

So Quinn was really the only child of mine I saw a lot of

growing up. I mean, Jesus, from the moment he was born and holding his tiny little hand in the oxygen tent to giving him hugs every morning before I left for work, I have been very involved with this boy. I had to be, he was in such need of us. He will always be in need of us.

I'm glad to be where I am right now. I don't have a ten-year plan. When opportunities come up that excite me, I do them, especially if it is something challenging. A few months ago I went to the Mideast and sat on a panel that spoke to eight hundred Arab journalists on American attitudes toward the Arab world. That was a lot of fun to do. And I'll go on Larry King or other shows when an important story comes up and they want my view. But when things come up on weekends, I often won't do them because I'd rather be with the family.

Being eighty-one feels bad in the knees, but it doesn't feel bad anywhere else. When on the land, I'm out in the woods five hours a day with my toys, my tractor and chainsaws. I love to find a little parcel that is overgrown with vines next to a swamp and clear it and plant it with something beautiful. Yeah, I really like this outdoor life, the guy thing. And I stay out there until I am physically exhausted. In the past, I didn't have the time to do that. I worked most Saturdays and Sundays.

I love this life right now, I really do. And, the love of my life is to be in the country with Quinn, which we've done since he was a child and he'd go out there with a tiny hatchet and we'd work together. His attention span was about twenty minutes; then he'd wander off and discover something else in nature. I used to go out in the woods with my own dad, but I am a much different father with Quinn than he was with me.

I mean, I wear my heart much closer to the sleeve. My father told me that he loved me once in his life, and he must have been sixty-five.

I remember exactly what I said back to him. I said: "I know that, Dad. I've known that all my life, and you don't have to say that. But I'm glad you did." And I was glad that he did, it meant a lot. I probably tell Quinn every day of his life that I love him. I hug him and kiss him all the time, three or four times a day. I never kissed my father much, that I can remember.

I've had no problem during my life going to shrinks if necessary. When you have a busy life it's good to stop for introspection and reflection. And I have always been reflective about relationships, especially if relationships go sour. All the shrinking I've done taught me that you have to talk your way out of the rough patches into an understanding of what caused them. This marriage works. Not only do we share this common preoccupation with Quinn, but Sally's in the news business. She loves what I love. That's been a great treat to have shop talk as pillow talk. Also for me, marrying somebody that much younger—Sally's twenty years younger—was marvelously invigorating. Suddenly I developed this new circle of friends in my fifties who were in their thirties. Even now, I have only a handful of friends older than me.

I'd like to think, even at eighty-one, that I'm continuously growing, yet I like that things have slowed some. I don't have to be listening to the television and suddenly hear something that makes me fly out of the house and go down to the newspaper at 10 P.M. and start on a story. I know who I am. Let's put it this way; I know enough about who I am, and maybe I don't want to know any more than this. Perhaps I have a sign somewhere still inside of me that says: "Don't go there." But I don't think so. I'm really quite open in a way that surprises people. I don't feel I have a hell of a lot to hide.

Obviously I think about dying, but I don't spend much time thinking about getting older because there's always some damn thing on my calendar that I have to do. The Quinn hurdles go on and on and they will for the rest of his life, and for the rest of my life. I can't think of anything I really desperately wanted to do that I haven't done. I wanted to write a book. I wanted to help the Washington Post be a great newspaper. I wanted very much to help Quinn shine. I've got all the damn houses I need. I've got a lot of good friends. I've seen the world. What else could I want?

To be happy in your life depends on how you adapt to the situation in front of you when problems arise. Do you adapt with resilience? Do you adapt with hope? And I've always had that. I'm hopelessly the glass-is-half-full kind of guy. Even with all the craziness in the world today, I don't worry much about being blasted into kingdom come. What can I do about it? I'm only interested in restricting my efforts and restricting my worries to things that I can do something about. Journalism is dedicated to finding the truth, and I guess in philosophical terms, I know my truth, what makes me the happiest. And that is to be in the company of people I love.

I'm not as overtly productive as I once was, but I feel good. I've got a fake knee, one is metal. But it's the only health *thing I've got. I'm in good shape. No, I wouldn't change much about this life. I would say the one constant for me has always been that I never stayed doing something that I really felt cornered by. I'm in a good marriage now, but in the last analysis, it is really your life, and you've got to find a way to make it work. And when it doesn't work, you need to fix it and get back on your feet.*

What God Can Do for You

Bradlee is an inspiration because he has held tightly to the reins of his life at every turn, and steered his own course of success over a period of eight decades. Yet I understand why many people get tremendous relief from the feeling that God is in charge, watching over them, taking care of their families, giving them strength on the job, keeping the devil from destroying the universe. "Let go and let God," friends tell me when they see me worrying about the health of my children or when I'm shaky about boarding a plane in a thunderstorm.

Well, I do believe God is with me, but I don't think God holds my reins. I actually think God doesn't want to be in control. God wants us to be in control of our integrity, our morality, our missions, our happiness. But God is as real to me as She or He is to those telling me that it's God's will that prevails, and not mine. I buy into the unifying principles of major religions: That God exists. That, through worship, the divine presence comes alive in our hearts. That death is a passage, and the soul is eternal. That spiritual richness, not material riches, is what makes for lasting joy.

Yes, I believe in and worship a God that is all-pervasive, a God that shields the universe, a God that is a steel floor upon which humans can dance and spar and make mistakes and go on. I love God, always have, since I was a child who kneeled at the side of my bed and said prayers at night, giving thanks for my family, friends, house, teachers, guinea pig. The last line of my prayers was "Please, dear God, help my parents live very long lives." And well, when my father died at sixty-seven because a doctor in Coronado, California, treating him for a coronary gave him an overdose of drugs that caused bleeding in his brain, I shifted my thinking about what God could do for me.

God is not a wizard who waves a wand and fixes whatever needs fixing, as I used to think when I was a young girl. God can't stop a bleed in the brain, and God can't hoist a crashing plane mid-air on his shoulders. Who, then, is God? If there is a God, why is there such hell on earth? The answer is, there is no answer; faith is not fact-based, it is soul-based.

During an interview, I asked Elie Wiesel whether he believed in God, to get a view from the concentration camp survivor who writes books of testimony on how bodies of children were "turned into wreaths of smoke" and has a blue A-7713 branded into his arm. And here's what Wiesel said: "I'm asking the question and there is no answer to the question. Where was humanity? And also where was God? I still wonder what was His role. Just as you cannot conceive Auschwitz without God, you cannot conceive it with God. And that's the trap, so what is the answer?

"I will continue to question until the end of my life."

Starting with Jacob, the God-wrestler, the Jews have always questioned, debated who God is and what is God's role in our lives. Yet even when I have doubted that God is real, I have always been placated by the consistency of the Jewish rituals, the predictability of our celebrations, the rhythm of our more than 3000-year history. After a lifetime of praying and searching and meditating, the God I've come to know may not always do what I want, but the spirit of the divine keeps my soul flowing everlastingly. God is the finger-wagger within that pushes me to do the right thing. My loving God makes me feel that when I'm alone, I am never really alone.

This is reassuring to a woman at midlife who lately never seems to go a week without hearing of someone I know who has been diagnosed with a grave illness or has died. At midlife, we must confront our mortality, we must accept that our family will leave us, that we are all we have. Knowing how God fits into your concept of self is essential, and I believe God is a friend you can make at any age, even if you've spent forty or fifty or seventy years as a disbeliever.

You cannot know who you are unless you know your relationship with God. Indeed, surrendering to yourself comes a lot easier by embracing a spiritual order greater than your own selfish desires. The God I don't know, and can't imagine ever knowing, is the one some people ask to help them come up with enough money so they can buy a Range Rover when they have an empty bank account. The God I don't know is the one people ask to find them a job when they haven't sent out any résumés and haven't gone out on any interviews. The God I don't know is the one some people think is in control of their lives and of the universe. God doesn't want us to hand over the reins. God wants us to figure things out for ourselves, using our best judgment, our highest moral code, by working our hardest, by being of godly character. The old adage is true: God takes care of those who take care of themselves. God is a force, not a face.

That doesn't mean we should stop praying because no one is listening. Prayer gives us clarity and calm, and from that place comes an increased ability to hear your own essence, your gut yearnings, your calling. When reciting this passage from Volume I of the *Union Prayer Book of Reform Judaism,* I know I am in dialogue with the Almighty: "O Lord, be merciful to us in our failings and trespasses and, when we have gone astray, help us to find our way back to Thee . . . We need Thy help, in our endeavor to fulfill the deeper longings of our hearts." That's my God, the one who puts me in touch with the deeper longings of my heart, and gives me the courage to take action on those longings, the courage to be weak and strong and real.

We all know friends who are certain that God doesn't exist. They say they have never felt God's presence, and don't need that crutch. When my uncle died, I told a friend that at last the deceased, ailing for years, was now with God, and that they were both probably looking down at us right now, grinning. This friend shook his head and said, "You know what a dead dog, rotting on the side of a road, looks like after he's been hit by a car? That's what happens when we die. Don't fool yourself." Living in rural Maryland, I've seen lots of dead animals rotting on the side of the road, from dogs to raccoons to skunks to deer. But no one can tell me I'm fooling myself when I tell them that I am convinced that our soul is eternal, and that God moves from this life with us into the next. God is in for the long haul, whether we choose to believe or not, and He or She does not leave us to rot.

I find my own passion for God when I read about the Kabbalists, the swaying, chanting Hasidic mystics hot on the trail of Holy Ecstasy. These are the soul masters who cartwheel to synagogue and swear God exists because they feel and live the Divine Presence in earthy, mundane daily life. Israel ben Eleazar, the Ba'al Shem Tov, who lived in eastern Europe in the 1700s, is credited with igniting the Hasidic flame of ecstasy, and making it available to ordinary Jews. The heart of this teaching is *devekuth*, or cleaving to God through celebrating the God in nature, in humor, in cooking, in all acts of everyday life. And from this place of divine awareness, cleaving to God while going about your business, can come the state of Holy Ecstasy, a joyful burst that is of this world, not beyond our reach.

Hitlahavut, or Hasidic enthusiasm, is described by Perle

Epstein in her book *Kabbalah: The Way of the Jewish Mystic* as follows:

> *For the Ba'al Shem Tov and his followers, enthusiasm was the proof of one's contact with the divine reality. Ecstasy occurred not as a result of arduous contemplation of the worlds within worlds, but as a spontaneous outflow of energy in response to* this *world and to the God who lives in its every stone, crawling insect, and child.*

In Elie Wiesel's book on Hasidism, *Souls on Fire,* here is how it feels for a Hasid to be ignited by the holy sparks from a master: "No matter how hardened, how icy your soul may be, at his touch it will burst into flames."

I am enamored with these believers who have God dancing in their hearts, a God who lives in the here and now, and who we don't have to die first to get to. I have danced with God, soul on fire, after rousing Friday night prayer services at our little temple in Anne Arundel County, Maryland. I have a dream about once a month in which shards of light shake me awake, and I get out of bed and look at the clock and it is always 1:26 A.M., eerily the precise time the hospital called to tell us my father had stopped breathing in early 1986. I believe that his soul left his body the second he died, and that he is dancing with God in an infinite circle of divine ecstasy, that he is what is called in the Bhagavad-Gita a Supersoul. I believe in luminescent angels who know everything. Being open to a radiant and divine presence or aspiring to reach a state of *Turiya*—Sanskrit for primal awareness—puts us in God's company, whether we believe or not.

"A human being is a spirit. But what is a spirit? Spirit is self," writes Danish philosopher Søren Kierkegaard in *The Sickness Unto Death.* The thought of men and women as spirit—fluid like the waves, airy like the wind, moldable like clay—explains our wafting emotions, our ability to transform ourselves, and is perhaps proof of our eternity. Spirit *is* indefinite, it does not die. And I believe spirit is shaped by God.

To know God and to know yourself, a person needs periods of perfect stillness. As Mother Teresa writes in her book *No Greater Love,* "It is only when you realize your nothingness, your emptiness, that God can fill you with Himself. Souls of prayer are souls of great silence.

"Because in the silence of the heart, God speaks. . . . Listen in silence because if your heart is full of other things you cannot hear the voice of God."

In our house of yelping sons and Frisbees flying through the living room and onto the piano keys, it is hard to be still and hear God. Yet away from noise and boys, I do hear a symphony of divine melodies, a thunderous chorus of silence, a hum from the soul. I become saturated in the Self that belongs not to me but to everything. You can, too.

Be still, really still, and listen, really listen. The barely audible vibration is the beating of your divine being, and the pulse of the universe. You can depend on the ethereal world. You cannot depend on the material world. My friend Tom Ferraro just called me to lament that after last night's thunderstorm, "we lost all our power," that his house is cold and black. Of course, he didn't mean power in the larger sense, he meant power as in electricity. But when we hung up I started thinking about the phrase "I lost my power," and how we often think we've lost our power when hard things happen to us, from wounding romances to ravaging weather. But real power has nothing to do with what occurs out there; power comes from what emanates from within. And through hurricanes and break-ups, we will never lose our power if we are illuminated by the light of God.

Joseph M. Forman, the rabbi of our temple, gave a provocative sermon a few years back for Yom Kippur, the Jewish holiday of atonement. He spoke about what spirituality should be, a godly force that makes us want to always put our finest, rawest, truest self on the line. These swatches from his sermon are a reminder to deem this day holy, constantly:

Yom Kippur is a day of baring our souls, unadorned, naked. A day of exposing all that we are and looking into our hearts to consider if today will be a day of renewal for us, a day made holy by our choices for tomorrow; a day we sanctify by understanding on this day the sacred power we can give to every moment in our lives. Listen now to the words of the Civil War poet Stephen Crane as he creates an image remarkably reflective of the mood of this day:

In the desert
I saw a creature, naked, bestial,

Who, squatting upon the ground,
Held his heart in his hands,
And ate of it.
I said: "Is it good, friend?"
"It is bitter—bitter," he answered;
"But I like it
Because it is bitter,
And because it is my heart."

Today is a day of sitting. Of squatting upon the ground, as it were, and thinking about our hearts. Is there one among us who doesn't know of what Stephen Crane speaks? Haven't we, too, sat alone with our hearts in our hands? Every year—perhaps more often for some—we imagine that we might change; that we might let go of worn-out dreams and abandoned hopes. Mingled with the sweet taste of hope may be a sense of regret and disappointment, a taste of bitterness at what the past year did not bring for us. . . . Seeking, searching can often seem like a never-ending struggle; a futile attempt to discover a joy, a sense of meaning and purpose that is just over the horizon. . . .

This morning, we are here as a community, looking; we are searchers looking for a way out of the forest. . . . On Yom Kippur, many of us spend the greater part of the day wrestling with these thoughts. How can my life matter? How can I find purpose in what I do, amidst all the mundane things I must do simply to survive? Where is the sweetness of my life? . . .

We know that this day is considered the holiest day of the Jewish year. But it is not sacred because the calendar says it is. It is not holy because the Torah tells us it ought to be. This day *is a sacred day because we have made it so. . . . So what then of other days? What of other places? Can't we take the power of this day and have it fill our lives, can't we bring a sense of the holy into every moment? If nothing else, on this Yom Kippur we can rise from our sitting with an understanding that a sacred occasion need not require a calendar or a schedule.*

When we feel the embrace of a loved one, we are experiencing Holiness. Whenever we put a piece of food into our mouths—or feed others at a soup kitchen—that moment can be a sacred event for us. Whether we are atop a mountain or at the shore, whether at the golf course or caught in traffic—anywhere we are can be a place filled with a sense of holiness.

We can make holy any day or any place or any moment—if we choose to. And perhaps, knowing that, is all we need to know to make our life a sacred journey.

THE SURRENDER

When I'm not carting children and their sports equipment, I drive a bright yellow Ford Escape—just got it a few months ago. My mom-car is a 1994 Suburban, teal blue, a tank with lots of dents. The seats and ceiling are crusted and mottled like an abstract painting from squirted juice boxes, mashed sandwiches, ink from broken pens.

A mother from my children's school, eyeballing our new vehicle in the parking lot, clucked at me yesterday: "Hmm, I see you are having a midlife crisis." And I told her that this car, chrome yellow, is hardly a crisis, but rather marks a midlife triumph, that the commercial tag line for the Escape is "no boundaries," and that's how middle age feels to me. In that car, alone, listening to the Dixie Chicks, I feel as if I'm encased in sunlight. The Escape brings out my teenage self, my California self, the selves I never want to lose. In fact, I go on to say to a thirty-four-year-old woman who I'm sure wishes that she had never mentioned a crisis of any kind, midlife has come to mean having more fun than I've ever had at any age or stage in my life.

That's how I'm feeling at the end of this book about celebrating and knowing fully who we are: Jubilant. Expectant. Shaken awake. As stated in my books on motherhood and marriage, this surrendering is not yet a fait accompli. But after a year of excavating my own self and dozens of others, I'm definitely farther along on the path toward knowing who I am, what I need, what dreams should be acted on, *now*. The resounding *ah-ha* I come away with is that our selves and souls must be solid and resilient to ground us in a world that changes in a finger snap. We are the tree that we must lean on; the tree is not something in the forest outside of us.

To wake up to our limits, our potential, our purpose, and our passion is the greatest gift we can give ourselves, to be lit from within, a light that shines on others. I'm thinking of people I know, you, too, know people like this, who have no light in their eyes: everything is a drag, the world's a cruel place. They tell you their spouses are awful, their bosses are dictators, their kids don't listen; they routinely send their food back when you are out to dinner with them. Nothing is ever right. They are victimized by life itself. And it's everyone's fault but their own.

Without fail, what you find when you peel away some of their layers in conversation is people who are disappointed in who they are; thus the world perpetually feels disappointing. I've been that person who was waiting for people to entertain me, to float my soul, to make me happy. With age, change, mistakes, and brutal honesty, I have found, as those I interviewed also discovered, that nothing will please you until you learn how to please yourself. That when you love who you are, life feels a lot more loving.

There is a cherry tree in our backyard that blooms for ten days in April, sometimes shorter if a storm blows through and eviscerates the conch-pink blossoms. It is the most astonishing of trees, the branches heave with color, and they jut and arch in a way that seems otherworldly, as if they were painted to illustrate the landscape surrounding a castle in a book of fairy tales. When spring comes, I cannot wait for the cherry tree to bloom, and the day it does, I sit before it silently, as if by an altar, stunned by its glory. For one and a half weeks, the cherry tree is noble and ripe, the god of the garden, infusing all who come and go from the house with a mystical charge, a sense that all is right with the universe. The flickering pink strikes somewhere so deep and pleasing you know it can be nothing else but an answer from your soul.

The petals are gone as quickly as they come, and seeing

the branches, barren of their babies, is genuinely painful, as if someone has died. In the eight years we have lived in our house I have been getting better at mourning their passing, the quick burst of poetry, after months of expectation, sumptuously present, then gone in an eye blink. I realize that I must not allow the vibrant pink of the tree to take me so high, because the letdown is severe, a spiral into gloom. So I have forced myself to become more clear at remembering how the tree makes me feel, and carry that memory throughout all the seasons. More and more, the bloom of the soul is still there when the branches are only brown sticks and twigs dripping with tiny icicles. My tree reminds me that we cannot rely on temporal nature or temporal people for our well-being, and that all is temporary, except for the bloom of the soul. I have grabbed at spring and grabbed at peak experiences in hopes of making them last forever, and fallen hard when they eluded my grasp. Nothing lasts but what blooms from within.

"We may lose the planet," a high-ranking U.S. government insider is telling me the day that there is much discussion of whether India and Pakistan will get into a nuclear war. The two countries settled off the battlefield for now, but there are eruptions large and small on many other continents. Some simmer beneath the surface like a dormant volcano; in Mideast countries there are continuous geysers of bloodshed. That we are already losing pieces of the planet is burning incentive to find ourselves now and "keep true to the dreams of our youth," as my fortune cookie says, to fan the bloom in our souls. In a fragile world that offers no promises, our promise to ourselves better be to love as deeply as we can, and to do as much as we can—now.

Composing this book on heeding gut passions and living urgently I am compelled to go back to California and spend time in Venice Beach, a haunt of my twenties that was bizarre and wonderful and at the roots of my old hippie self that never died, and will never die. I take Theo with me to California, who decides when he's there, although he is only in seventh grade, that he wants to go to college in Los Angeles, because he likes the atmosphere. On the Venice Beach boardwalk, aflame with sun on skin on a Sunday afternoon, his mouth drops open as he gazes at the vendors lined up along the beach farther than he can see, selling brass urns and tooled wood furniture and dried herb wreaths, offering Tarot and palm readings, Chinese massages. We stop at a tattoo booth and Theo looks at me with pleading eyes, and I say sure, get one, after the artist tells me his henna designs last only a few days. So Theo now has a two-inch dragon on his upper right arm, and I am thrust back to Venice circa 1970s, when I bought the long skirts and long earrings and gauze shirts I still have, and where for a dollar, street artists would paint a daisy or peace sign on your face.

I am thrilled to be sharing this Technicolor circus with my adolescent son, artistic fervor and abandon he's never seen before. On Venice Beach, Bohemian is not just the look du jour, the latest chic of polyester paisley blouses that cinch below the breasts and low-slung jeans that come torn, and aren't torn out of years of wear. I'm showing Theo the place where Bohemian is a life, where Bohemian may have been born. In central ways, it's where I was born. Strolling amid minstrels, fortune-tellers, skateboarders and falafel stands, I see how the seeds planted in me here circa 1975 are responsible for some of that bloom of the soul today.

We venture off the boardwalk onto the beach, weaving our way through an Ultimate Frisbee game, and sit down in the downy sand. "I love California," my twelve-year-old whispers. And I tell him that what he loves is how it makes him feel, and that he must never forget this feeling of being 100 percent alive, from unrelenting sun, kiosk after kiosk, character after character, of houses tucked into overhanging cliffs and old hippies making a living selling crafts they create lovingly with their hands. Most of these folks are poor in the bank but rich in their souls. I am thinking about the grown-ups I know who make a lot of money but have no passion, they are sleepwalking through their lives.

In Venice Beach, you are slapped awake, forced to pay full attention, or else you will get run down by Rollerbladers in Oakley shades, or shirtless old men, walking with their eyes closed, playing the banjo.

We stop at a stand selling vintage black-and-white photographs lacquered onto squares of pine, and I buy a portrait of a Native American maiden shot by Roland Reed in 1915. The picture, called *Proud Heritage,* depicts a young woman in side profile, solemn and beatific, her black braids secured by a beaded headband that circles her forehead. I can't take my eyes off the picture as I pay $10, for this turn-of-the-century Indian princess who seems like a lost friend.

"You know, you lived then, that's why you are drawn to her," the vendor tells me, a woman of about sixty with skin like leather, and long gray hair secured by a beaded headband across her forehead. Her eyes are clear green and they aren't looking at me, they are looking through me. I shudder because, as I said earlier, I have always thought that the desert Southwest is where my ancient self took form, and I tell the woman about my soul-deep love of turquoise and silver and horses and Arizona. She nods, staring like a sorceress, and keeps saying, "I know, I know, I know."

I grab Theo and we move quickly away, because this divine wackiness is about all I can take right now. As was the case a quarter century ago, Venice Beach still holds the power to push me to the edge. Stretching beyond familiar ground is good for all of us, to leave behind what is known and safe. When I was twenty in Venice Beach, a palm reader told me I would have four children, but not until I was almost forty. I thought she was nuts. Our third and fourth children were born two months after my thirty-ninth birthday.

My eyes are open just a little bit wider after our sojourn through Southern California. I'm recharged—the bizarre can be invigorating. When I lived in California as a college student, I would often feel a complete opening of self, from the cliffs and hills and the force of the ocean waves, from the eucalyptus and bougainvillea, from seventy-two-year-olds with chiseled abdominals, from people who perceived no boundaries.

I return to the East Coast and am aware that many people back home clutch their spirits to their chests, wary to out their full-bore selves. But a soul needs to fly, only then can we achieve the freedom and audacity to do things others might snicker at, but that feel indisputably right.

A month ago I was having lunch at a patio restaurant on Capitol Hill, and a man in a blue blazer and gray pleated pants Rollerbladed past me. He had loosened his tie, and it was tossed over his shoulder, and he was sweaty and smiling, oblivious to how he may have appeared to passersby. Instead he was focused on getting some exercise and how the wind felt on his face. This guy had Venice Beach in him, in a city renowned for repression. We need to be free, to let our spirits out of cages, to let our wild children within be a constant source of surprise to us and to others. That is living.

What place on the planet gave you a charge in your youth? Go back there, recharge, fan the flames that have been snuffed with time. If you're sleepwalking and operating at 25 percent, travel to the place where you felt the happiest, wake yourself up, grab your joy back, and bring it home. Give yourself a jolt.

Planning a trip to get your self smoldering again means you are living intentionally, making things happen, not letting your life be something that happens to you. You have the power to create a mosaic of self in which the pieces of history fit together in a well-integrated pattern, representative of all sides of you, not thrown together randomly. You can get what you want if you know what you need and you are willing to work hard and take chances.

I'll tell you what I don't want: I never again want to feel like my life is disingenuous, as it has felt in certain crowd-pleasing turns along the road. When I turned forty-five I stopped caring what other people thought of me. If someone ruffles me I tell them so, and I expect straight honesty from others. I wear what I want to wear, and if someone reacts with a cluck of the tongue, I smile broadly, staring them dead in the eye. In my writing, more and more I am willing to say things that some readers may find offensive. I don't censor my sentences in my brain; they come straight from the heart. Trying to please everyone just waters down your own self. No longer do I go places or accept invitations because I feel like I should; I'm too old to do things because I should do them. I do things because I want to, and I do what is right for me to do, or work that serves others. I also make sure that part of each day is spent doing something fun, that I laugh. Our son Jack was recently in a swimming pool with Chuck, and I overheard him ask "Daddy, why aren't grown-ups ticklish?" Chuck answered, "I don't know, Jack." And to that Jack replied, "I know why; because grown-ups are too busy to be ticklish."

Never be too busy to be ticklish. Stop long enough in this moment to let fingers flicking along your body make you giggle, or to be tickled by the whimsy you may be missing by zooming, head down, through your life. When we are present with our senses and not numbly focused on what comes next, we will laugh more, and that opens up a soul like nothing else.

I relate to the protagonist in Colin Wilson's book *The Outsider,* someone who continually prods and pokes for answers to life questions. This can be a tough and painful undertaking. Wilson describes the symptoms of *The Outsider*: "An immense confusion bewilders me. . . . I see too deep and too much." Yet digging deep beneath the veneer of convention and social games is necessary to find truth of self, and to manifest your full creative expression. The work of many of the most accomplished artists and writers reveal a penetrating and pained search for truth, from Vincent van Gogh to Franz Kafka to Bob Dylan to Lily Tomlin.

Coming of age at the onset of feminism left my generation of women ablaze with ambition, and I used to have quick, sure answers when asked about the meaning of life: The meaning of life was for women to gain equality. Outraged over how masses of smart mothers throughout history ended up shackled to their homes, I was driven to be a master in the world, never a slave to a kitchen, husband and kids. As a journalist who specialized in celebrity profiles, I have sat at the table with lots of movie stars, senators, a king, and a queen. Yet famous people and world travel didn't form my core of self; it was the frosting, sweet and swirly, but not the cake.

After years of interviewing subject after subject, I knew a lot about everyone else but not enough about myself. I didn't morph into my real self until I had that husband and house and kids I once believed to be the death of dreams for a woman. With a family constantly in your face, mirroring your good sides and your bad sides, you have no other choice than to be your fullest, most truthful self.

I am reading in *Parade* magazine a quote by Tyne Daley,

the Emmy-award winning actress from the old series *Cagney and Lacy* who now plays the opinionated mom on *Judging Amy*.

"There is a period when you wish you were Meryl Streep, but then you get over that and you are comfortable with yourself," says Daley. There is a period in all of our lives, if we're honest, when we want to be someone else, perhaps someone as beautiful and talented as Streep. But then you get over it, you relax into yourself, and realize that who you are is enough.

If it's not enough, do something about it, become larger, learn something new. A startling discovery that could add zing to your old bones may be right outside your window. I grew up around lots of birds in my backyard in Illinois, but they were just birds to me, I could identify a robin and a crow, but that was about it. Two lucite bird feeders filled with sunflower seeds hang outside our kitchen window in Maryland, a state that is a sanctuary for wild bird life. All day they attract a swirl of birds, all kinds of species. Our older sons did an intensive study unit of birds in school, and I have become their rapt student, who can now identify scrub jays and cardinals, the American goldfinches and blue jays and Carolina chickadees that peck at our feeder. My new bird watching hobby is not yet at the level where I spend hours in the woods with binoculars waiting for a bald eagle. This ornithological odyssey is conducted while sitting on the couch in my kitchen, the *Audubon Guide to Eastern Birds* in hand. But I'm still captivated, ebullient, to be learning something new, to have kicked open a new door in the corridors of self.

I am remembering a conversation I had with pilot Wesley Jones when I asked his advice on getting over my fear of heights. This man who crashed in a plane, then went back up two days later, told me something I'm holding on to: "You can't touch the clouds when you're on the ground."

This morning I was driving on the Chesapeake Bay Bridge, and the wind was so blustery there were whitecaps on the water. My car was shaking, and so was my gut. I looked over the edge at the 186-foot drop to the water and panic knotted every nerve. This renowned Maryland bridge is one of the highest and longest in the country—a four-mile span—and many people with fear of heights drive hours out of their way to circle through Delaware, then back into Maryland so they can avoid it. Others take advantage of the police escorts available at the tollbooth; cops who will drive you across while you crouch down on the floor of the car, head in hands. I've never had an escort, and I cross that bridge often, to buy seafood from local watermen, to horseback-ride, to visit Chuck's family. On sunny days I have no problem, lulled by the panorama beneath me, the rushing water dotted with sailboats, yachts, ferries, fishing cruisers, and barges of goods headed for the harbors of Baltimore.

But in bad weather, it is terror that rocks me, not the scenery.

On this windy day, I looked up at bulging gray clouds. The sun was trying to push through, so that it looked as if the dark clouds were outlined in fire. And that incandescent light show just calmed me, I didn't think of falling, I thought of rising, as I did standing on a peak of the Grand Canyon. After this experience, I cross the bridge once a week now whether I have to get to the Eastern Shore of Maryland or not. It is my exercise in conquering a fear that I am ready to be rid of forever. When that's gone, who knows what other layers of self can emerge?

Fear, or lack of fear, is at the root of who we are and who we become. I was watching MSNBC, and a journalist friend, Marie Colvin, was being interviewed about the Mideast conflict, which she was covering for the London *Sunday Times*. Back in the eighties when I was a feature writer at UPI, Marie was a reporter on the foreign desk, and we hung out a lot after work. She is smart, fun, and fearless, a tangle-haired beauty who is always up for anything. Over the years, Colvin has become one of the most formidable war correspondents in the world, treading turf in Chechnya and Kosovo and Afghanistan and Iraq where few reporters dare to go.

A recipient of the Best Foreign Correspondent in the British Press and The American Women in Courage Award, Colvin is to print journalism what Christiane Amanpour is to the broadcast media. Single and childless, she is simply unstoppable, no matter what happens. In April 2001, Marie was hit by a grenade in Sri Lanka that blew out vision in one eye and cost her nearly half her blood supply, but in spite of her shrapnel injuries she still made her deadline, writing a 3,000-word report on what had happened there. She had traveled to a war zone to interact with the Liberation Tigers of Tamil Eelam, something which is banned for journalists.

Under Sri Lankan law, journalists must obtain written permission from the government to travel to rebel-held areas.

After several months of healing, Colvin, wearing a black patch over her dead eye, is back on the battlefields. Asked by the MSNBC reporter what made her return to the war zone, she explained without hesitation that war is about people, and to cover the story right, you have to get "inside the story" and talk to the people in the middle of the war.

I always admired her absolute courage; I used to wish I was Marie Colvin, a journalist who will travel anywhere and interview anyone, however dangerous is the mission, because of her compulsion to tell an important story and to muckrake truth. I don't know any other person like her.

I run into reporters from my old UPI crowd around Washington, and conversation always turns to "Did you read about Marie?" I've often heard the remark that Colvin must be out of her mind; that after nearly getting killed, she should go get another life. But I watch her on TV and read about her adventures in magazines like *Vanity Fair*, and I am convinced that picking herself up and going back to work was her only choice. Colvin could go get another, safer life, but it wouldn't be her life. What she does is who she is, and however horrific are the scenes of her day, she operates out of passion in her soul, and that is what we all should aspire to. She is doing what she needs to be doing, she knows who she is.

Who am I? I am Iris, an unabashed homebody, drawn more to the living room fireplace than the arsenals of war. I crave security with the same fervor as other reporters crave chaos. And my purpose, and greatest adventures as a journalist involve soul travel, not air travel. This is okay; it is what I was meant to do, just like war reporting is what Colvin was meant to do.

What were *you* meant to do? Real freedom comes from knowing who you are, by being awake as the self evolves over time, so you know to stop when you land in the right place. I think back on the years I kept busy to run away from myself. You can't find what you're looking for while you're on the fly. When you're always searching, you're never finding. It is natural to admire others, but to want their lives is to miss out on your own. To be present with who you are, to live passionately and love wholly—that simple formula is at the heart of happiness.

It's Mother's Day, and after the family fussed over me this morning, my gift from Chuck is that he took the four boys out for the day, across the Bay Bridge, to go visit his ninety-seven-year-old grandmother Mattie. It's early evening, and I'm sitting on my porch in the house that I hope I live in for the rest of my life, eating sardines from the can, lightly smoked, skinless, bathed in olive oil, just how I like them. It's only me, and the river, and a couple of squirrels fighting over some seeds that have dropped beneath the bird feeder. I sit for a long time, in gratitude, for this home and these kids and this Chuck, and the salty taste of the sardines.

I know that everyone doesn't live on a scenic river and that some people hate sardines, but it strikes me how simple it is for anyone to steal a perfect moment in which you realize how lucky you are to be who you are. The next day I am early to pick up the boys at school, so I park my Suburban at a nearby playground, sit on an empty swing, and start pumping my legs faster and faster, until I'm high enough that the bars of the swing set are swaying from the weight. As I'm winding down, a young mother with an empty stroller in one hand and a blanket-swaddled infant in her other is singing softly to her child. I am remembering all the nights when I would sing softly to our babies, or put them in car seats in the middle of the night and drive around the block, or plop them on top of the vibrating clothes dryer—the times I'd do anything so that our children would sleep. What young mother isn't ready for her baby to be still for a while so she can have some stillness to herself? What changed people we become when our children get some years on them and we have that peace we were wishing for, but it turns out to be hollow, haunting, until we figure out how to fill it, with pieces of self that have been sleeping.

Today, my four sons each have one friend over, and eight boys are seated around the kitchen table, waiting for lunch to be served. I am grilling cheese sandwiches, and I've got two pans going, because each child wants two sandwiches. Some want American cheese, others want Swiss, and one kid wants Muenster. Yes, I was stupid enough to give them a choice. And I'm huffing and red-faced, like a short-order cook in a diner, as I serve up the goods, pour eight glasses of milk, and sprinkle potato chips on each plate.

They are teasing each other about girls, imitating teachers, talking with their mouths full, and there is such gorgeous bedlam that I have to leave the room, because while they are whooping with laughter, I am starting to cry. I'm fast-forwarding to that day a few years away when I won't be taking grilled cheese orders and taking care of everybody, but it will be just me mothering me, alone in the house, eating what I want, when I want, or not eating at all because of a stomach knotted from missing my old life when famished kids were always around.

This verse from Krishnamurti speaks of what will be gone: "There was a blessing in the air, a love that covered everything, a gentleness that was simple, without calculation, a goodness that was ever-flowering." Goodness flowers, and overflows over us, all the time, and as we racewalk through the rat race, too often we miss it, it's gone and we wonder where we were while it was there. Days should not be blurred; they should be stark, vivid, palpable, there are too few days not to rejoice in each one. So be fully there while you're there, but prepare yourself for the next life around the corner. Because what is now won't be then; the only certainty in the world is what you hold inside of you.

This truth is glaring at dawn today as I am writing on September 11, 2002, one year after the morning that shook us all awake. However far you live from the killing fields of Manhattan or Washington or Pennsylvania, no one escaped the stench of death and the agony of loss and the wrenching realization that we get one life, and one self, and that's it. Loving, and being loved, by our family and friends is a healer and a joy that is ours only now—we cannot depend on tomorrow.

Knowing this is an opportunity to get to a place where

your heart opens to the vastness of the sky, to a God-force, in surrender and gratefulness, and the self becomes every-thing. With the universe in your heart, when death whispers the names of those around you, you will carry on because the stars carry on. Although saddened and shocked, you will still have passion and you will still own your soul, which no one ever takes away. I love my husband, Charles Anthony, so, so much, he's given me everything. But I am Iris Kras-now, the same name on my birth certificate from Edgewater Hospital in Chicago.

In a letter from New Mexico in the early 1900s to her friend Anita Politzer in Texas, Georgia O'Keeffe wrote:

> *I walked out past the last house—past the last locust tree—and sat on the fence for a long time— looking—just looking at the lightning—you see there was nothing but sky and flat prairie land— land that seems more like the ocean than anything else I know—there was a wonderful moon—Well I just sat there and had a great time all by myself.*

We should all be moving toward a plane where we, too, can have a great time all by ourselves, looking at the sky, lying in the grass, no people, just our heart songs. Yes, that's it.

Bibliography

Angelou, Maya. *Wouldn't Take Nothing for My Journey Now.* New York: Random House, 1993

Barclay, Shinana Naomi; Lamb, Gaia. *The Sedona Vortex Experience.* Sedona: Quantum Leap, 1987

Bradlee, Ben. *A Good Life.* New York: Touchstone/Simon & Schuster, 1995

Brehony, Kathleen A. *Awakening at Midlife.* New York: Riverhead Books, 1996.

Camus, Albert. *Notebooks 1935–1942.* New York: Hamish Hamilton and Alfred A. Knopf, 1963

Collage. The Attic. Chicago: Writes of Passage, 2001

Dass, Ram. *The Only Dance There Is.* New York: Anchor Books/Doubleday, 1973

Easwaran, Eknath. *Climbing the Blue Mountain.* Tomales, Ca.: Nilgiri Press, 1996

Ellis, Neenah. *If I Live to be 100.* New York: Crown, 2002

Epstein, Perle. *Kabbalah: The Way of the Jewish Mystic.* Boston, London: Shambhala, 1988

Estes, Clarissa Pinkola. *Women Who Run With the Wolves.* New York: Ballantine Books, 1997

Gunther, John. *Death Be Not Proud.* New York: Harper & Row, 1949

Gyatso, Geshe Kelsang. *Introduction to Buddhism.* London: Tharpa Publications, 1993

Housden, Roger. *Ten Poems to Change Your Life.* New York: Crown, 2001

Joy, Charles R. (edited by). *Albert Schweitzer: An Anthology.* Boston: The Beacon Press, 1947

Kierkegaard, Søren. *The Sickness unto Death.* New York: Penguin Books, 1989

Krasnow, Iris. *Surrendering to Motherhood.* New York: Hyperion, 1997

Krasnow, Iris. *Surrendering to Marriage.* New York: Talk Miramax Books, 2001

Krishnamurti, J. *The Book of Life.* HarperSanFrancisco, 1995

Markham, Beryl. *West with the Night.* San Francisco: North Point Press, 1983

Miller, Arthur. *Death of a Salesman.* New York: Penguin Books, 1976

Peale, Norman Vincent. *The Power of Positive Thinking.* New York: Prentice-Hall, 1952

Proust, Marcel: *Remembrance of Things Past.* New Haven: Random House, 1932

Schachter-Shalomi, Zalman, with Donald Gropman. *The First Step: A Guide for the New Jewish Spirit.* New York: Bantam, 1995

Sheehy, Gail. *New Passages.* New York: Random House, 1995

Teresa, Mother. *No Greater Love.* Novato, CA.: New York Library, 1996

Tyler, Anne. *Ladder of Years.* New York: Fawcett Books, 1996

White, John. *A Practical Guide to Death & Dying.* Wheaton, Ill.: Theosophical Publishing, 1980

Wiesel, Elie: *Souls on Fire.* New York: Touchstone, 1982

Wilson, Colin. *The Outsider.* New York: Jeremy Tarcher/Putnam, New York, 1982